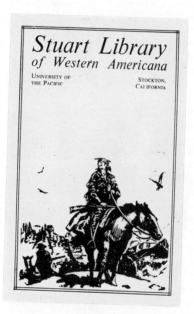

Six Thousand Miles of Fence

NUMBER ONE

The M. K. Brown Range Life Series

The M. K. Brown Range Life Series

Six Thousand Miles of Fence IS THE FIRST BOOK TO BE PUBLISHED BY THE UNIVERSITY OF TEXAS PRESS IN THE SERIES WHICH HAS BEEN ESTABLISHED THROUGH THE GENEROSITY OF MONTAGU K. BROWN OF PAMPA, TEXAS. HIMSELF A PANHANDLE PIONEER, MR. BROWN HAS LONG BEEN INTERESTED IN PRESERVING THE RECORD OF HIS REGION AND OF THE MEN WHO MADE IT. ADDITIONAL TITLES IN THE SERIES WILL BE ANNOUNCED SOON.

R. L. "Bob" Duke, the last XIT general manager
to run cattle. The time is 1912.

6,000 Miles of Fence

Life on the XIT Ranch of Texas

By CORDIA SLOAN DUKE

and JOE B. FRANTZ

UNIVERSITY OF TEXAS PRESS, AUSTIN

International Standard Book Number 0–292–73379–8
Library of Congress Catalog Card No. 61–10042
Copyright © 1961 by Cordia Sloan Duke
All Rights Reserved

Manufactured in the United States of America

Sixth Printing, 1972

TO R. L. (BOB) DUKE
*and the men and women who made the
largest fenced ranch in the world,
the* XIT

Preface

In 1907 Cordelia Jane Sloan married Robert L. Duke, a ranch hand who had risen to division manager for the 3,000,000-acre XIT Ranch of Texas, the world's largest. An eager observer, she early began the habit of keeping a diary. As time passed, she had the foresight to realize that the sweaty, tired, hungry cowhands with whom she visited were part of a unique phase of American life. What she particularly perceived was that these men would be glamorized and the memory of their work distorted by writers who could sense a pay vein when they saw one.

Besides keeping her own diary, she encouraged these cowhands—some barely literate, some with a fine sense of communication, but nearly all of them men who could go months or even years without taking pencil in hand—to jot down descriptions of what they did as cowboys. This way, she felt, some later generation could know what it was like to have been a hand on a vanished ranch in a vanished era. Through her own drive and enthusiasm she persuaded these nonwriting men to write at length, straightforwardly, without apology. Sometimes their reminiscences were little more than a recalling of names and faces, but many others contained detailed job descriptions by the men who actually did the chores, and who were able to describe their jobs in a manner and with a completeness that may well be unique.* Eventually almost eighty cowhands—or, in some instances, their wives or sisters—responded.

As the decades rolled by, Mrs. Duke added to the roster of reminiscences. Occasionally she did a short piece from these resources for *The Cattleman* or for some newspaper. But by and large she merely waited until about a year ago, when she suggested to the University of Texas Press and me the idea of making the sketches into a book. We were both enthusiastic. Even if we had been uninterested, she probably would have charmed us into wanting to work with her. But we had already made up our minds before we fell under her spell.

What follows is in no sense a sociological tract or a simple job description. Nor does its purport to be a history of the XIT—J. Evetts Haley and Lewis Nordyke have presented that story far too well to leave need for additional versions. Instead, Mrs. Duke and I wish to let the XIT cowboy tell the story of his workaday world as he saw it, stripped of the false heroics imposed by countless Hollywood and TV scenarios and many more thousands of "Western" storytellers, who

* And then there is the case of Andy Jones, an XIT hand who told his daughter some of his ranching experiences. When she used part of this material in a story for her high school class the teacher commented that either Mr. Jones or the girl had a vivid imagination. From that time forward Andy Jones had nothing to say.

may operate out of Liverpool, Los Angeles, or any other "Western" point in between.

The authors of these sketches shared one common experience—somewhere in their careers they had been associated with the XIT. Before or after they worked for the XIT, they worked for other outfits—or, in some instances, for themselves. We have made no attempt to confine their story to the one big ranch, but to draw from their experience wherever it was enjoyed, or endured.

In the main our function has been to moderate, to announce the next speaker, and then to get out of the way. At times we have debated whether the editing should be tighter, but when a cowpuncher was wound up and making good sound, we were disposed to let him go on "cooling his coffee,"—to use a favorite cowboy expression—even though what he was saying might stray a bit off the narrative range.

Along the trail we had some assistance. From what I can gather, everyone in the Panhandle would have liked to help Mrs. Duke, but those to whom she, and I too, owe an especial debt are those XIT men and their feminine partners, some a long way over the Divide, who took the time to remember.

And from my end of the corral I should like to thank particularly Mrs. Duke's daughter, Mrs. A. B. Warrenburg of Houston; Dr. Llerena B. Friend, Texas History Center Librarian, the University of Texas; Mrs. Tita Garner of El Paso; and Miss Suzanne Kain and Mrs. Gretchen Blackmon of Austin, all of whom assisted in some necessary way. I am grateful also to the Research Institute of the University of Texas Graduate School for its material aid. All photographs which do not carry credit lines are from Mrs. Duke's personal collection. Paul T. Armitstead of Austin drew the maps. And finally I want to thank Miss Colleen T. Kain, who acted as a sort of subeditor, not only wielding an intel-

ligent pair of scissors but assisting also in selection and
organization of material, so that the cowboys did not trip
all over their spurs as they sauntered through my mind and
vision.

J. B. F.

Cordia Sloan Duke

Late in the afternoon I dismounted from my bus in the high-plains town of Dalhart, Texas, and crossed over to the appropriately named XIT Motel. As I signed the register under "Firm Name" my host, reading upside down, said, "University of Texas—what department?"

"History," I said.

"Then you will want to see Mrs. Duke while you're here."

Later that night while I was strolling around town, tasting the wind as it kicked up little eddies, a former student hailed me. After the first amenities had been exchanged, he said, "You know, you should see Mrs. Duke while you're here."

Before I went to Dalhart I had corresponded with Mrs. Duke and had talked with her on the telephone. Somehow I had pictured a gaunt, raw-boned cowman's wife, face leathery and seamed by the sun, voice rough and language rougher. What I found the next morning was a genteel little woman, the perfect portrait of a sentimental grandmother, dressed in taste, with a wide-ranging interest and a feeling for the cultural side of life that contrasted strikingly with her story of having homesteaded as a barely grown girl, of having threatened an intruder with a gun, or of having fought dust and blizzard a hundred miles from anything that in the usual sense could be called civilization. I found too a woman of eighty who was attending writers' conferences, submitting her own efforts to professionals for criticism, and in general seeking to learn to write, all with as much hope and indefatigability as if she had been a lass of twenty with a half-century ahead of her.

I learned that Mrs. Duke had been writing for nearly fifty years. As a young ranch wife she had begun a diary. Busy as any mother of three with a herd of cowhands to look after, she had carried a notebook and pencil in her apron pocket and had written at every opportunity. When nothing happened to add to the diary, she would reach back to jot down recollections of her childhood. "I got the habit of writing, and I couldn't stop," she said.

In the 1920's she nearly stopped. Returning from placing her daughters in Lake Forest College, she confided her writing ambitions to an actress riding alongside her. When Mrs. Duke told the actress she had been married only once and had three daughters, the actress was disappointed.

"There are millions of women with one husband and three to six children. Now if you had had three husbands and one child—"

Mrs. Duke was born Cordelia Jane Sloan near Belton, Missouri, on January 10, 1877. Her mother wanted to name her Lena Rivers after the novel, but as so often happens, duty to grandmothers prevailed. On her mother's side the family were Illinois Dunkards, which meant they had opposed the Civil War, or, for that matter, any war. When grandfather found a coil of rope on his front doorstep, he knew that he was out of harmony with his neighbors, the more especially since he usually voted Democratic. And so he had moved to Missouri. Shortly after Cordia was born, her father moved the family over the line into Kansas, despite a cousin's admonition that Kansas "will be the ruination of you."

The Sloan family was as independent-fibered then as Mrs. Duke is now. Her grandmother, Jane Alcorn Sloan, had left her Kentucky home, ill with chills and fever, on a feather mattress strapped to a cow's back. At twelve her Uncle Byron attended a celebration at the school in which those present cheered for Lincoln, then Grant, Sherman, and Sheridan. Suddenly young Byron arose and shouted, "Hip! Hip! Hip! Hurrah! Three cheers for Jefferson Davis!"

Instinctively the entire audience cheered—and then stopped as suddenly as if their breath had been sliced off. The school board met on the spot and expelled Byron from school, but not without asking him whatever had possessed him.

"Wasn't Jefferson Davis a big man in the war, too?" he asked.

With that, an angered mother took her three children, including Mrs. Duke's mother, and placed them in a Catholic school in Independence. The children never became Catholics, but in their adult lives they always provided overnight hospitality for any Sisters of Charity that might pass through their town.

"We have never been known for riches," Mrs. Duke said, "but rich people did not pioneer in this country. It took people poor in this world's goods but wealthy in religion, truth, and honesty.

"Well, you say, isn't that conceit for you! But if you have

ancestors like that, you have a considerable chunk of this world to live up to. That will take the conceit out of you. People that are trying to live up to a heritage may be self-trustful, but never conceited."

One ancestor that always puzzled Mrs. Duke was her father. As she grew up, she never received any affection from him. "I always thought it was because I was a girl," she said. "My father had been the center of attention in his family, as he was the youngest of eight children, five of them girls. I was the first person to move him out of the center. Being a girl I was of no value." She was in her forties before she learned that the real answer to the puzzle went back to the time when, as a baby of eight months, she had been taken to a doctor.

"The doctor said that if this place burst outside I would get well, but if it burst to the inside I would die and the doctors could do nothing. Mommy put me in my father's arms as they were getting out of the buggy at home. He hurt me and I fainted. My mother began to cry, 'You've hurt her!' "

In 1919 Mrs. Duke's father told her that after her mother had charged him with hurting Cordia, "I never touched you again."

While she was still a child, Mrs. Duke's family was swept up in the fad of psychic phenomena that intrigued the nation following the Civil War. Although her father believed that death was the end, he couldn't resist the temptation to try to communicate with his dead parents, four sisters, and a brother. He and others also believed that his wife was an automatic writer.

It was not uncommon therefore in the Sloan household for the family and friends to gather after supper, put a lamp on the shelf by the Seth Thomas clock, and hold a table-tipping séance.

"In some old messages that I have," Mrs. Duke averred, "I know that if my mother had been trained she would have been a writer. These messages, which show what a forceful subconscious mind she had, were far different from her ordinary writing; in some of her own writing she was timid, but in these she gave commands meant to be obeyed. As to these messages coming from people that have passed on, I have my grave doubts. But she honestly believed that they were from the departed, and so did everyone else.

"My father had a brother William in Nebraska City, who dismissed these séances with 'It's of the devil.' In the light of what has happened since, along the years, I agree with him."

Whatever the state of séances, Mrs. Duke definitely is not "of the devil." Since the trip to Dalhart I have seen her elsewhere, and we have exchanged more letters. I see readily why people in Dalhart told me I should call on her. Her conversation is invariably sprightly and bright. She never falls into that mannerism so annoying to a listener, of retarding her story to search through her mind for a date or a detail; she roves all over the time-scale in her talk; and she switches without warning from personal reminiscence to strictures on Texans who voted against Al Smith and on to instruction in the proper way to brand a steer. Described in baseball parlance, she has a tremendously effective let-up pitch, and she mixes her stuff beautifully.

She leaves me feeling more than a little humble.

J. B. F.

Those Who Remembered — and Recorded

Pres Abbott
Nils M. Akeson
J. W. Armstrong
W. A. Askew
J. S. Beasley
Bob Beverly
Jack Bradley
W. T. Brown
Mabel Buckley
Myrtle Buckley
Charles H. Burrus
J. H. Childress
Ina Chillcut
W. J. Cook
S. R. Cooper
Mrs. Will Corder

J. M. Curry
Earl Davis
A. L. Denby
L. L. Derrick
Tom Dixon
Robert Dudley
Steve Dugger
Mrs. C. S. Duke
Robert L. Duke
Gene Elliston
Ed Faubion
Walter Farwell
H. Field
George Findlay
Roy J. Frye
G. E. Glidewell

Fred Graven
C. H. Hanbury
Mack Huffman
Ed Jeffries
Worth Jennings
Bob Johnson
Andy Jones
Tom Jones
J. S. Kenyon
Lee Landers
John Lang
Ed MacConnell
J. K. Marsh
Col. Robert McCormick
Charles McNeil
L. D. McMakin
J. H. Meeks
Emmett Mims
W. L. Molyneaux
Mrs. Bessie Montgomery
J. H. Montgomery
J. Ealy Moore
Walter Moore
Mrs. Ernest Morris
Jesse Morris

Mrs. Lydia Morris
Jim Oden
J. G. Owens
W. W. Parks
Jake Pitts
W. E. Price
Albert Roberts
Alec Sevier
Frank Shardelman
Jordan Shaw
J. A. Smiley
Arch Sneed
Allen Stagg
R. J. Stallings
J. W. Standifer
Blue Stevens
J. W. Stewart
Mike Tafoya
Goldie Thomas
T. A. Turnbow
W. D. Twitchell
Joe Webb
Mrs. Allen M. Willbanks
Jack H. Williams

Contents

List of Illustrations

List of Maps

Six Thousand Miles of Fence

THE RANCH

TEXANS IN THE 1870's cherished the same illusions that they still cling to nearly ninety years later—that Texas should have the largest and greatest of whatever was worth the effort. And one item that was worth the effort was a new state Capitol which should be larger than any other state capitol building in the United States and taller than the national Capitol in Washington. The only difficulty with realizing that desire was that such a building would cost money, and in the 1870's and early 1880's the Texas Legislature was dominated by economy-minded Grangers, none eager to spend public moneys or to raise taxes.

There was, however, a way out. By the treaty which

brought Texas into the Union and other settlements of the
next decade the state retained her public lands, so that in
the period following the Civil War Texas still had millions
of acres to dispose of. Since so much of the public land was
in that semiarid section known as the Panhandle and was
not likely to attract individual buyers within the immediate
future, the state liked to grant the land in that area to encourage railroad building or similar projects. To the state
government the land was so much dirt and grass, isolated
away beyond the fringe of civilization. On the other hand,
money was hard come by. The logic therefore was irresistible:
contract to have a Capitol built, but pay for it with land,
which is plentiful and practically worthless, instead of with
money, which is scarce and dear.

The result was that in 1882 the Sixteenth Texas Legislature appropriated three million acres in the Panhandle, to
be allotted to whoever would build a suitable state house.
The information was broadcast throughout the United States,
and even from abroad inquiries were received, but when
the deadline for bids had passed, only two bidders had come
forward. Apparently the prospect of becoming the owner of
the nation's largest tract staggered and frightened most
land-hungry Americans.

But not one group of Chicagoans. Without going into the
intricacies of their individual arrangements, suffice it to say
that Mattheas Schnell received the contract to build the
Capitol, shortly transferred three quarters of his holdings to
a group that came to be known as the Capitol Syndicate, and
then sold the other quarter to the same group.

The Capitol Syndicate was composed of John V. Farwell,
Chicago's largest dry goods wholesaler; his brother, Charles
B. Farwell, a congressman who had helped organize the Republican Party in Illinois, had sponsored Lincoln for President, and seemed likely to follow him up the trail to the

White House; Amos Babcock, another prominent Republican office maker; and Abner Taylor, politically inclined but better known perhaps as the chief contractor in rebuilding Chicago following its Great Fire a decade earlier. Taylor would build the Capitol; the others would supply the business and political sagacity necessary to carry off an operation of this magnitude.

In a way it is incredible that a quartet of hardheaded Midwestern business and political figures, none of them with a ranching background, would undertake to run a spread in size three times the largest one in existence today. Further, that with their supposed acumen they would obligate themselves to build what at that time was one of the nation's more expensive edifices is equally fantastic. And when you consider that for payment they were taking land which none of them had ever seen, land a hundred miles from the nearest railhead and almost as far from the nearest outpost that could pass for a real town, and that they were going into the cattle business full tilt, without any attempt to build slowly, the improbabilities increase.

Like good businessmen, the Farwells, Babcock, and Taylor intended for their ranching enterprise to pay. Furthermore, they intended to use their gigantic holdings to settle the country. They would be ranchers only so long as the land could not be utilized for other purposes, especially agriculture; but eventually they planned to subdivide, become a land-selling syndicate, and get out of ranching. How many years it would be till "eventually" they had no way of knowing.

Since to stock the ranch required more money than they had readily available, the syndicate formed the Capitol Freehold Land and Investment Company, Limited, in London, selling bonds to the English, who had already invested heavily in the American cattle industry, but who nonetheless were willing to risk their capital in one more enterprise. By 1885 the steps in making the start had been taken, Abner Blocker, a trail driver of considerable experience, had devised a brand and given the ranch a name, and word had been sent to Texas cattlemen that the XIT was buying.

By November, 1886, more than 110,000 cattle had been purchased for 1 1/3 million dollars. From that time forward the XIT maintained about 150,000 head on its 3,000,000 acres, trailing cattle to the northern buyers in Kansas and elsewhere, operating a finishing ranch in Montana for some 10,000 head annually, and in general conducting a full-scale ranching enterprise.

There was, of course, more to running a ranch than raising money and raising steers. From the beginning the XIT was placed more and more under fence. In the first year alone 781 miles were fenced; each year this total was increased until finally the equivalent of 6,000 miles of single-strand fence were strung—enough fence to run from New York to Los Angeles and return, and still have several hundred miles left over.

Fencing was not instituted so much to keep intruders out as to keep XIT cattle at home. Within the first few years the Farwells and their associates began a policy of controlled breeding, introducing Hereford, Shorthorn, and Angus to upgrade or replace the scrubby Texas cattle which they originally purchased or bred. By 1900 the XIT consisted of seven divisions with ninety-four separate pastures, each with its particular purpose.

Despite the care and organization that went into the operation, the XIT was slow to show a profit, and when the profits did come, they were insufficient to satisfy the English bondholders, many of whom had held their bonds far beyond maturity with no prospect of redemption. Faced with receivership, the syndicate decided in 1901 to begin selling its land wholesale. The first purchaser was Major George W. Littlefield of Austin, who bought 235,858 acres of the Yellow Houses Division. By the end of the year nearly a half million acres had been sold for more than a million dollars. With those sales and with each subsequent sale the number of cattle was reduced, until by 1912 the XIT was no longer in the cattle business. From that time forward the syndicate interested itself almost exclusively in colonization and development until by 1950 the Farwell heirs retained only twenty thousand acres—or less than .007 per cent of the original tract.

In the nearly seven decades of its existence before 1950 the XIT had seen the vision of the original partners of the Capitol Syndicate realized. The nine counties, plus the thin slice of Cochran County into which the XIT lapped over, that composed the ranch had become fine agricultural acreage, with good yields of wheat, cotton, and sorghums. The area still had spaciousness, but 100,000 people now lived where formerly 150 cowboys and a handful of foremen, women, and children had been the total population. Railroads and highways crisscrossed the ranch area; women met in Wednesday study clubs and men in Chambers of Commerce; and law and respect for order had replaced a morality sometimes enforced by strong-arm methods. Civilization, whatever that is, had marched on.

" . . . we got the full benefit of dust, smoke, and noise"

WORK

WHEN 150 COWHANDS and their 150,000 cattle and more thousands of horses filled the rough rectangle— almost 200 miles long and averaging 27 miles wide—that made up the XIT, what was their life like? Ranching, even in the 1880's, was not all horseback riding, trailing cattle to Dodge City, or heading a stampede. When you read or listen to the serious reminiscences of the old hands, you perceive that these men thought of themselves first of all, not as knights on horseback, not as romantic half-tamed champions of freedom, but as workingmen, as men who put in long hours for small pay, who knew the monotony of routine, who knew the weariness of protracted exposure,

who went from September to Christmas without haircuts or
baths, and who in later days hurt with every change of
weather because of broken bones improperly set generations
ago. In those decades between 1885 and 1912, what sort of
work had they done?

One answer can be found in the writings of W. A. Askew,
who as a scantling of a lad in Marble Falls had often listened
to the blasting of stone for the new state Capitol fifty miles
away. Askew went west to the XIT when he was not quite
twenty-one. His first few days were filled with odd jobs,
and then he was given a man's assignment—rescuing cattle
bogged in the quicksand. It was wearing work, tedious and
a bit dangerous.

"We soon found," remembers Askew, "that it was best
when a cow had to be pulled out of the sand to rope her
around the neck, because we could pull their horns off. We
had plenty of bog-pulling to do. When a cow got her hoofs
under the sand she could not pull them out and stand up
too. We had many trying experiences in this place."

When the boss came by and told Askew to break camp
and head for ranch headquarters, Askew had just one comment:

"I was glad to get where we had a cook."

R. M. Dudley worked the bog season alone during succes-
sive spring seasons in the 1890's, often pulling out as many
as five cows in a day from the Punta de Agua or the Rito
Blanco.* Heel flies were especially bad those years, causing

---

* Several names of places on the XIT defy precise and definitive
spelling. For some there may be a pure spelling, but often, even for
these, there are local corruptions. Also, many of the cowboys, being
of Southern extraction, were wont to slur their word endings, thus
confusing the spelling still more. For example, "Rito Blanco" is
found on some maps as spelled here, is seen on others as "Rita
Blanca," and was most often pronounced by the cowboys as a com-

the cattle to run to any mudhole and stand there most of the day to protect their heels. Charlie Burrus once saw thirty head bogged in an abandoned tank during heel-fly time. When the cattle would start to leave, the cows would find that they were effectively chained down, and could only wait till some bog rider happened their way. If the bog rider did not come in time, then the steer became a statistic, for an animal left overnight would become so chilled that he would not likely live even if rescued the next day.

Dudley's procedure was to scratch round and remove sand from one leg at a time, as, in his words, "the quicksand would settle and become solid as a wood floor." Once he had the animal out of the bog and to its feet, he would catch it by the tail and pull it to whichever side the animal tried to turn, always keeping the animal's head and horns away from him. "Usually a few back-and-forth turns like that and the animal is ready to go straight away; then the cowboy can mount his horse and ride on looking for another unfortunate victim."

Trying to reach water rather than rescuing cattle from its treachery was the chore of another hand, Bill Benson, who chiefly drilled wells.

"In some places," recalls Nils M. Akeson, "it was hard to get water, but Bill had the patience of Job and would hammer on a boulder for a long time to keep the well hole straight. One time he was drilling a well west of the Har-

---

bination of these two spellings, "Rita Blanco." The same confusion exists with the word "Alamocitos," spelled also as "Alamositas," and in other variations. In each such instance I have been forced to be arbitrary and to take a stand for consistency's sake. In some cases I would be hard put to defend my position, as all I seem to have done is to touch off controversy among members of the University of Texas Spanish Department and between the members of that department and the official makers of the map of Texas. JBF

rington Dam in a Yellow Houses pasture, had been there
for some time when we came along with our outfit to build
a tank, expecting the well to have been finished. Bill said
he was going to make a well out of it. Well, we risked his
judgment. It was to be a small tank and we would lose time
going and coming back; so we went ahead and built the tank
and went on our way. However, in a few days, the foreman
of the ranch wanted Bill to leave that place for the time and
go over in the Silver Lake Pasture and drill a well there, as
it was badly needed.

"Bill did so, and it was about a year before he ever returned to finish the well. . . . But he made a well out of it
and it stood the test and he got his pay for the well and we
received the $125.00 for our tank."

J. S. Beasley rode track. The Fort Worth and Denver
Railroad, which slanted across a Buffalo Springs pasture of
the XIT, was not fenced in the 1880's and was responsible
for any livestock killed on its right-of-way. "The track had
to be rode every other day," and then Beasley would ride
another fifteen miles to Farwell Park to turn in his report.

"In riding this line," writes Beasley, "I very frequently
came across wolves, and one morning I came across an old
wolf and four pups at an old carcass. I succeed in killing the
old wolf and all the pups."

No mercy was shown wolves, for next to fire, rustlers, and
drouth, they were the dreaded enemy, often with two boun-
ties on their scalps from both the county and the XIT.
Hunting lobos—or "loafers," as they were more commonly
called—could be a means of picking up extra money. Again
it was lonely work, far from the chuck wagon and far from
companions. When R. M. Dudley quit the XIT in 1896, he
started wolf hunting for the LE and LS spread in Oldham
and Potter counties at $35 a month. In addition, he was to
receive $5 a scalp from the county. His ranch furnished

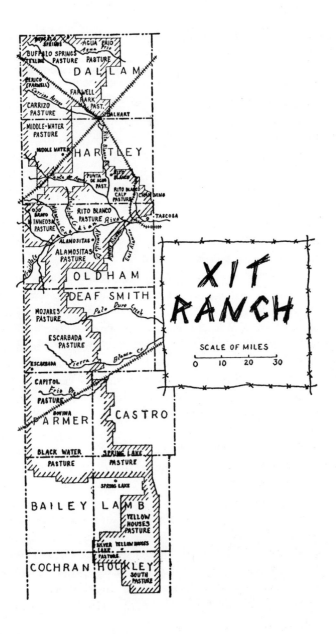

everything—food, eight horses in summer and four in winter, two rifles and a Colt .45, and all the ammunition he could shoot. Once in a while he was called off his hunting for cow work, but mostly he just rode and hunted.

On the other hand Charles H. Burrus looked on lobo hunting as a sport, and if he could get close to one while on a good horse, in a spirit of high jinks he would try to ride down the wolf and rope him rather than shoot the animal. The certain bounty was secondary to the chase and the catch.

Not so lonely but considerably more wearying was the work of branding. Blue Stevens didn't actually get into branding on his first job for the XIT, but his work laid the foundation for the branders. Stevens gathered cow chips for twenty-one straight days, picking up "enough . . . to brand all the cattle in Texas, I thought."

At the Buffalo Springs camp in 1888 J. S. Beasley met with about fifteen other hands, including two ropers, two bulldoggers, two men to handle the irons, and two men to use the knife (for earmarks, and so forth). Together they started for the pasture to brand, the chuck wagon following behind with instructions to stop on a familiar knoll for lunch.

"The riders were to prowl the pasture," remembers Beasley, "and bring all the calves to a certain slope and hold them in a bunch while the workers did the branding. As a calf was finished, he was cut out to a bunch of his kind; then they were all turned loose at the same time." Usually several hundred head were rounded up at a time.

John Land, who worked for the XIT before the Oklahoma territory was opened to white settlement, writes in some detail of the procedures of branding, as well as the wandering nature of some roundups.

"When a cow and calf were cut out so that the calf could be branded," he recalls, "the brand on the cow was

examined and the cow's calf was branded identical with its
mother. If an outside cow, the brand was usually a 'running' brand on the calf. Some of the ranches sent 'outside'
men as far as three hundred miles away to attend other
roundups. Many of the cowhands at that time carried branding irons on their saddles, the handle of the iron being short
for convenience and the brand in the form of a J so that it
could be used for a 'running' brand on any maverick they
chanced to come across. This was later made illegal in Texas.

"One of the fresh things in my memory is that I gathered
several mossheads. They were steers six or seven years old
and wild as deer and had the habit of making their gitaway
from the stray bunch after night. So I got Joe Tate, Cross
L man, to help me and we need them to do this. We would
catch these mossheads and cut the cords of one of their front
legs and through these efforts I turned several mossheads
and many other XIT cattle back on their home range.

"There were several notable events on that general roundup when I worked for the XIT's. The day of the roundup
near the headwaters of the Cimarron there came up a hail
storm on the east side of the Rabbit Ear Mountain that killed
a sheepherder and two thousand sheep. The hail fell to the
depth of about six inches. The next day the boys roped a
bear and brought it into camp. They had caught him in the
brakes of the Cimarron. From there on down Ute Creek to
the Canadian River we had such men as Charles Carson with
us—a son of Kit Carson, the noted scout. Also Crawford,
the poet who wrote the poem of Mady Coleman. This Mady
Coleman was supposed to have thrown a bouquet of flowers
into the Canadian River and dared her lover to go and get
it for her. He died in the attempt.

"Crawford wrote:
> 'She will juggle you in the palm of her hand
> And throw you headlong into hell.'

"And as the roundup drifted down Ute Creek Roy Lackey joined us. He was the boy who had been sent to college in the East by his folks and when they sent him enough money to come home on he spent it, so had to walk home. But when he had arrived in the cow country he borrowed a horse, a bad one of course, but when Roy rode the horse and fanned him with his Derby he had before him the cheapest bunch of cowhands you ever saw."

S. R. Cooper, who was "neither a writer of stories nor portry," came to the Spring Lake Division of the XIT in 1890, along with a brother and an uncle "that was hauling cedar posts." Let him tell his own story:

"I had my bed and saddle just looking for a job at that time. I was just sixteen and had never worked on a large ranch but had a desire to be a cowboy. My home was in Mobeetie at that time. Well, as we drove up to the ranch there were about sixteen or twenty men at the corrals and were branding and dehorning 1100 head of cattle they had purchased from a northern ranch. They were mixed cattle or what we call stock cattle from calves up to eight or ten years old and they were branding and dehorning in a large chute, sawing the horns off with handsaws and chopping the old bulls' horns off with an ax, as the saws were too slow for the hard horns of the older bulls.

"Well, we stopped there and watered the team and I inquired about a job and one of the boys pointed to a medium-sized man and said 'There is the boss.' So I went to ask him for a job and was informed the job was there. I drug my bed and saddle, which was an old Texas cack that had seen several years of service, and I started in. It was a hot day and the dust was bad as the 1100 head of cattle milled in the pens south of the branding chute and cows lowing, and calves bawling and bulls bellowing until you would have to holler

to make a man hear you, that was right at you, and before
you got your mouth shut again it and your throat would be
filled with dust and smoke from the burning hair, for the
air or what little breeze there was, was from the south. So
we got the full benefit of dust, smoke, and noise of it all
but I was enjoying it as I was now a cowboy and on a big
ranch.

"Well, about the middle of the afternoon I was sweaty
and covered with dust, as well as all the rest of the boys,
but I was not used to it, and I was a little too hot, and I
drank some of the good cold water just fresh pumped by one
of the windmills, and I began to feel dizzy, and I could not
hardly see; so I crept under one of the wagons standing there
loaded with prairie coal. This was the fuel they used in the
eighties to heat their branding irons with and also for cooking. Well, I lay there for some time and felt bad, and I was
afraid the boss might fire me the first day, but I finely
crawled out and went to work again handing hot irons to one
that stuck them on (done the branding) and I would put
the cold irons back in the fire to get them hot again.

"Well, the first day finely past, and my bunk bed felt good
to me that night, but my brother and uncle was to come
back by in about three days and I had begun to wonder if I
had not better return home with them to Mobeetie. But they
came by and I did not get to see them, so was just there with
saddle and bed and not even a horse of my own. So it was
up to me to make the best of it and besides I was a little more
reconciled. When the boss, Mr. Frank Yearwood, sent me
with a man to work on wells and windmills, but I did not
know much about well work, so I could hardly make a hand
at that. We were out about ten days on well work and came
back to the ranch for repairs and we stayed at the ranch two
or three days and he left me there as we had already learned

to dislike each other; and the boss's brother, Mr. Yearwood, let me help him hoe some corn, and I and another boy milked the cows. In a few days the chuck wagon and the boys and the boss came in by the ranch. They had been branding calves in the pasture that belonged to the No. 6 ranch, and when they left the ranch on another branding trip I was taken along and gathered up prairie coal for the cook and to heat the branding irons with. I used a team and wagon for this purpose and some days when I had time I would help wrangle horses or help day-herd the saddle horses [loose herd]. They also had to stand night guard over the saddle horses and I was rung in on that job. Some two hours was considered the time for each to stand guard."

It is not surprising that young Cooper did not make a hand at windmilling. Many cowboys did, but few actually wanted to, as it was one of the lonelier jobs, a sort of solitary unconfinement. Ina Chillcut, the younger sister of Tobe Pitts, foreman of the Buffalo Springs Division in the 1890's, recalls seeing the walls and doors of these line camps filled with bits of prose and poetry written by cowhands eaten by loneliness and boredom. Sometimes, she says, you would run across sentences on walls that hadn't seen a human being in years.

Earl Davis oiled windmills—"about forty or fifty"— along the New Mexico border. His most vivid memory, however, is not of the work involved, but of the winter he spent in a windmill camp in the northwest corner of the Middle Water Pasture.

"I was very young and that camp was so lonesome. While I was there they stopped in for dinner. There was the Blanks family and the schoolteacher, Mattie Technor, and also Donnie Bell, and we sure had a time getting dinner, which was beans, bacon, prunes, and sour-dough biscuits and black coffee. They were just coming from Buffalo Springs. They had been up there for Christmas to spend a week, and Tobe Pitts gave a big dance and dinner. The girls was telling me about it. I sure enjoyed their visit."

The feeling of isolation also looms large in the reminiscences of Roy J. Frye. Working out of Yellow Houses headquarters between 1893 and 1898, he first rode line, greased windmills, and looked after fence. The next year he worked with the cow outfit, wrangling horses. But the winter he cannot forget was the one spent fifteen miles from the headquarters ranch:

"I stayed in camp nine months by myself and sometimes I wouldn't see anybody for eight or ten days. I looked after the cattle in that pasture, the South Pasture.

"I've done everything on the ranch; went up trail to Channing a number of times. Plowed fireguards and helped burn them out and helped fight prairie fires and helped brand calves. I've seen lots of wild mustang horses and hundreds of antelopes, and while working there I roped a wildcat and I still have its hide.

"I married in 1898 and me and my wife went to the Yellow Houses Ranch and cooked at the headquarters. The ranch had a meadow about fifteen miles north of the headquarters and I helped put up hay and helped haul hay to the headquarters."

What looms largest in Jack H. Williams' memory of windmilling is not the replacing of wheels or the building of towers, but the team of horses that helped him and Ben Johnson in their repair and upkeep rounds.

"Our team of horses was the best for this business that I ever saw. Sierra Grande was a long gangling black horse that knew more about what he was doing than most of the fellows who tried to drive him. His mate, Good-Eye, was a big dap-

pled gray, blind in one eye. He didn't know so much, but he
went along with Sierra Grande, and did his part when it
came time to pull. We pulled sucker rods and pipe, and
raised towers with this team, and I marvelled at what we
could do with two horses.

"Pulling sucker rods was a snap. We would fasten the
blocks up in the tower and hook on to the rods, and maybe I
would drive the team the first two or three pulls, as there was
considerable weight to a string of sucker rods in a 300-to-
350-foot well. Then after that, we just wrapped the lines up
on Sierra Grande's hames, and I worked up in the tower, and
Ben on the ground. Each time a rod came up Ben would sing
out his 'Who-o-o,' and the team would turn and come back
to the tower, ready for another pull."

As with Frye, windmilling was only one of a variety of
chores for some of the hands. J. W. Armstrong remembers:

"My first job was the plowing of ground for the planting
of sorghum for feed. I was a freighter for one year freighting
supplies of salt, chuck, hay, windmill supplies, in fact anything needed on the ranch, from Farwell Park [Perico] and
Channing to Middle Water Ranch. I windmilled for four
years and looked after thirty-six mills on the Middle Water
Division; later I drilled twenty wells in the division: Buffalo
Springs, Rito Blanco, and Middle Water."

Another odd-job man was Jack Bradley. "I worked at anything that was to be done," he recalls. "Windmill helper
a while and then run the windmill wagon a while myself.
Cooked several times a few days at a time. When any cow
work was to be done I was with them also, fencing, haying,
and tanking, and in 1897 the last trail herd that was ever
driven from the XIT I helped to gather that."

But no one progressed from one ranch job to another with
the combination of zest and truculence of a hand whose

name, Blue Stevens, could have been invented in Hollywood. Stevens did dirty work—he once complained that he had "picked up enough cow chips to heat branding irons for every cow in the U.S.A.," and he did deadly routine; but to him it was all a challenge and an opportunity, and his account reads as if he reveled in every moment:

"My work was all kinds: pick up chips, wrangle horses, cow punching, drove a freight wagon, plowed corn, the last a funny pice of work. My boss, Mack Huffman, told me to take my team hitch to a plow he had fixed just like he wanted it. I did, plowed all day and the cultivator had three plows on it; so there was a streak all through the field of weeds. Five cowboys had to hoe, and, well, the boss couldn't tell until the next morning what was wrong or played on him. Mr. Boyce, our general manager, was there to see us start work. When we run the cultivator under the shed Huffman said, 'Blue, did you plow that corn with one plow off?' I said, 'You're getting $75.00 per month to tell me what to do. I am getting $25.00 to do it.' Mr. Boyce told him I did him right.

"My boss, Mack Huffman, sent me to Amarillo with a freight-team wagon, a six-mule team 'jerk line.' I never had no experience in freighting. The boss said when I went to load my freight, 'Hook up four mules,' which I did. I had the wrong mules in the lead. So I went to drive up to the drugstore to load on a barrel of oil, when the leaders [mules] saw the wagon-yard gate open, and went in the yard, tore the steps and porch off the drugstore. The men come to help me out and said I had the wrong team in the lead. I soon discovered that. They, the men, wrote the boss his freighter had torn up everything.

"When I got in to the ranch the boys helped me to unhitch so they could have the mail. I wouldn't let 'em have it until they did.

"The Boss said, 'Blue, what did you do in Amarillo? The man wrote you tore down everything in sight.' I said they told the truth.

"I learned to paint, freight, plow without a plow, drive six mules with one line.

"I forgot to tell about running the mower—that was expensive experience learning a cowboy how to mow hay. I did not know how to get the sickle in the guards; so with Jo Anderson's help we went to cutting the guards off with a cold chisel. We cut for one half a day and the boss, Mack Huffman, come to the camp. The first word he said to us was, 'Cowboys, what are you doing?' I said, 'Fixing to put this sickle in the guards.' He showed us in about five minutes how to raise it up and push the sickle in. That shows you what 1890 cowboys knew about farming. We knew nothing about that but did know how to round up cattle and string them out on the trail.

"These modern cowboys string their herds in trailers. That is the reason cowboys today sing the old trail song, 'Roll on little Dogies,' where the old-time cowboys sang, 'Go on little dogies, for Montana is your new home, for it is your misfortune and not my own.'

"My first trail herd work was in 1886. Joe Ferguson boss of the herd. We drove this herd from twenty-five miles south Fort Worth to Schleicher County, Texas.

"I was in Ballinger, Texas, when the first train came in. I come in on the first train that come into Seymour, Texas; we had a big ball in the courthouse that night.

"In 1889 I come to the Fish Ranch. It was sixty-five miles from Midland, Texas, and that was my postoffice. We got our mail not by air but by freight wagon. What would these eastern cowboys do? Sing a lament song, 'I am going back to Mother; she has a feather bed.' It took a boy with 'guts' to

stay in those days. Those that stayed were the best cowboys I
ever saw. I loved them all.

"In McCullough County before I worked on the XIT we
held a herd at the head of the Colorado River in the Long S
range. We had a corral to pen the cattle in, but those bulls
would get back in the herd in the daytime and we would
cut them out every night when we went to pen. Cutting a bull
out of a herd was a dangerous job. They were Spanish bulls,
and would hurt a horse.

"There were lots of cactus in that country; so we would
rope the cactus, pull it up by rope, get the cactus by the root,
and sling it on the bull's back. Say, cowboy, that bull made a
lane through the herd of cattle, never come back to our herd
no more.

"When the Long S outfit rounded up at the waterplace
where we was holding the herd Red Beach was wagon boss.
When he rode in to cut out the calves to brand, the bulls all
ran out. Red and those 'peelers' went after the bulls but
never brought them back.

"The boss rode up to the Rafter T man, Frank Shelton,
and said, 'Cowboys, what have you done to those bulls?'
Frank said, 'We just cut them out of the herd.' Red Beach
said to Frank, 'It takes a fool on a race horse to head them
bulls.' "

For variety of experience J. W. Standifer could run Blue
Stevens a close race. Standifer took more than a score of
pages to exhaust his reminiscences, most of which are scattered throughout this book. In this small excerpt we get
some idea of the gusto with which Standifer met the frequent
fickleness of cowboy fortune, the sudden switching of as-
signments, and even the caprices of Panhandle weather:

"Next morning every one was assigned their various jobs,
and mine fell to cutting dead cottonwood into stove wood. It

was like cutting sponge—ever time my ax hit it bounced back. I held this mean job for two days. Then about six or eight of us were loaded into a four-mule wagon, headed for Buffalo Springs, about one hundred miles north. Frank Owens and a man named Jones are the only names of the men I can recall now, except the Negro Hal. One pair of the mules had never been hitched up before, and were as wild as deer. That morning before we could get them hitched up they jerked Jones down in the grass burs, and he even had burs in his hair when he got up. We drove forty miles that day, and our mules were almost given out when we turned them out that night at Middle Water.

"Next morning bright and early we started on the sixty-mile end of our journey and arrived at Buffalo Springs that night with a much gentler team of mules.

"There had recently been a prairie fire that had burned out a lot of fence posts on the eastern string of the Buffalo Springs Division fence. About six or eight of us were sent out on this job, with a camping outfit, to repair it. Among the men besides myself were Joe Adams and Bob Roebuck. I remember this trip especially well, as I got my first experience with 'graybacks' [cooties] while on it.

"We were on this trip about ten days. Another severe snowstorm blew up while we were out. I had never been in very many, and didn't have sense enough to be afraid. But Joe Adams had presence of mind enough to make us dig a hole in the ground. It wasn't hard to dig in the sand, we dug it to the depth of about ten feet, and large enough for us all to get in, with a small fire in the middle.

"Next morning everything was covered with snow, and the wind still blowing a gale, but the sun was shining. So we went back to work. And during the day I had the misfortune to lose my hat—the wind whipped it off my head and simply blew it away. I was forced to wear a flour sack tied round my

head for two days. On the third day we ran into some windmill men, and one of them had an extra cap, which he gave
to me.

"We worked hard, but when one is young and healthy you
get a lot of excitement and fun out of everything.

"I wish I could recall just half of the amusing and exciting
things that happened. I remember a little incident that happened about this time. Four or five of the boys, including myself, were riding along about halfway between Buffalo
Springs and where Dalhart is now and we rode onto about
fifteen head of buffalo. We gave chase and one of the boys, I
don't recall his name, caught a calf. We tied it down and
tried to catch another but were unsuccessful. And when we
got back the one we had tied down had gotten away. I guess
we were so excited that we didn't take time to tie him well
enough.

"In December, 1888, I drew my pay and headed for
Burnet County. I had worked nine months, and only spent
$5.00 of my wages.

"April 12, 1895, I began work again on the XIT Ranch. I
was quartered at Rito Blanco, and I remember it was so cold
that seven or eight bulls froze to death right out in front of
the barn, only a day or two after I got there. J. E. Moore was
division boss then and the longhorns had been somewhat
thinned out, and replaced with Polangus and Hereford pure-
blooded stock. All the longhorns were kept on the Rito
Blanco division. Alamositas [Little Cottonwoods] was the
Black Muley Division.

"In 1897 and '98 Boyce got us boys to take up claims on
the school lands that was fenced in with the XIT Ranch land.
And the company would give us twenty-five cents an acre for
it after we had proven up on it. This was to keep out nesters.

"In the winter we boys were put out in line camps, usually
by ourselves. Two winters I stayed in a little 'dobe-and-rock

shack, called Cheyenne line camp. I rode fences and bog—
lots of the cattle would get in the quicksand along the Canadian River. Also lots of the creeks had bog holes on them.
In the early spring the heel flies would run the cattle in the
creek and lots of them bogged down. It was a hard job for
one man and horse to pull some of them out, too, if they
were in very deep. Moore had Walter Prestiss to ride bog in
a wagon one winter, Walter said that was the funniest way he
ever saw anyone ride bog before. I was living by myself, but
an old man named Johnnie Mack lived about half a mile
from me, and raised a garden and some chickens. I got one of
my horses choked to death one night, so Johnnie Mack
skinned and cut off a hind quarter and took it home for his
chickens to eat. He hung it up and each day he'd cut them off
some of it. One day we had both been gone all day, and
when we got to his house some one had cut off a big piece of
the horses' hind quarter. We never knew who it was, but he
evidently took it for a nice fat beef's hind quarter.

"We also branded a few mavericks while in line camp,
which reminds me of what happened to Duke one winter. He
was camped at Alamositas, about twenty miles from where I
was, but we often met. One day I met him and he was the
worst bunged up fellow I ever saw. He had been trying to
brand a maverick, and some way he had gotten wound up in
the rope between the horse and steer; he said he wasn't able
to ride for several days. We always had plenty of good eats,
especially since Duke was boss. The wagon always had all the
beef it could use and in winter they fattened seven or eight
spayed cows. In that country beef kept without any curing
even in summer."

Whether the job was astride or afoot, concerned with laz-
ing turtles or insistent bulls, most of the hands felt pride in
merely belonging to the XIT. W. J. Cook expresses it this
way:

"It was in the spring of 1887 that I drew into camp at the Alamositas, a part of the XIT. The trail herd of the OB cattle belonged to Snyder's of Georgetown, Texas, in charge of Duck Arnet. Colonel [Barbecue] Campbell was general manager at the time and Billy Ney was ranch boss. Ney put me to work the day I pulled in. I was pretty proud of that too. It meant a lot to me that a big outfit like the XIT would hire me on the first deal.

"The first four days I ran branding irons on the branding chute. We branded several thousand head; we knew how to work in those days, and we didn't dilly around either.

"It was spring on the range, and you know what that meant. Well, just after we finished that job Bill Ney sent me to New Mexico to work with the general roundup. We started in at Seven Rivers near the Pecos and worked up the Pecos River. We worked through the Lightning Rod, the VN, the Jingle Bob, LFD, the ꓷꓷꓷ, and some more ranges. We wound up somewhere around Fort Sumner. I left for the ranch with 185 head of XIT cattle and turned them loose in Silver Lake Pasture.

"Things were changed up quite a bit when I got back. A. G. Boyce had taken Colonel Campbell's place and Billy Ney was gone. Frank Yearwood had taken his place as boss of my division. I worked with Yearwood's wagon there through the fall and early winter. There had been an extra amount of cattle brought in that year, bought in the South. Spring Lake and Yellow Houses pastures were packed. We had to drive part of the herds north to the breaks in the Alamositas."

After that began some real work.

AND MORE WORK

EVERY MONDAY MORNING the six-mule freight
team and its trailer would set out from the XIT, heading for
Amarillo, the nearest rail point, eighty miles away. If all
went right the cowhands would be standing with their backs
to the Saturday sunset as from the east the faithful old team
would come creaking down the hill into the headquarters
yard. If the freighter had happened to think of it, he would
have picked up the mail—if there was any. He definitely
would bring news and gossip, of which there would be some.
As for the cowboys, they had spent the interval between
Monday dawn and Saturday sundown working at familiar
tasks, chores so automatic and repetitive that the return of

the camp tomcat from a two-day search for companionship could be as absorbing a conversational topic as a visit to the United States by a Russian dictator is today.

Lee Landers worked like this on the Rito Blanco Division for four years, riding line, bogging, plowing fireguards, rounding up cattle, haying, fighting fires, feeding cattle, and freighting supplies.

"It fell to my lot to stack hay every summer when haying time came," [he writes]. "The first summer I was on the ranch, in 1900, they poured it on me pretty strong, but in 1901 I had a little help. It was that summer I started the longest hay stack ever seen on the Rito Blanco Division. It measured seventy steps in length.

"The last year I was on the ranch I was made foreman of the farm about a mile and a half south of Channing, known as the 'Poor Farm.' We had between seven and eight hundred acres in cultivation and our crops ranged from wheat, maize, and hay down to 'pie' melons.

"In 1902 I was one of five men sent to Montana. Each of us was in charge of a trainload of cattle. I do not recall the name of one of the men but remember the others. They were George Young, 'Pope' Carpenter, now dead, a man named McMiken, and myself.

"One day I was riding a horse called 'Cornstalk' about two miles northeast of Endee when I jumped a big lobo wolf. I took down my rope and roped him. I didn't have anything to kill him with but my rope; so I doubled it up and beat the wolf to death."

None of the hands has written more fully of his life on the XIT than J. S. Kenyon, who joined the ranch in the early summer of 1887. Although his narrative rambles considerably, its very discursiveness points up the variety of experience that many cowboys enjoyed. A part of Kenyon's long story follows:

"About the first of December [1892] I went in to winter quarters on the Escarbada Division in a tent not far from Mojares Canyon but down next the Mexico line not far from [where] the Trujillo line camp was afterwards put. They had a deep well and windmill, [as well as an] excavation and troughs.

"They had fifteen windmills and excavations at most of them, and of course, troughs, and tubs at some of them in place of troughs, sixteen feet in diameter about two and a half or three feet deep. Then they had some reservoirs built by building a dam across a draw and taking most of the dirt from the upper side, thereby making it considerable deeper reservoir and of larger capacity.

"At the time, 1888–1893, they had some on North and South Palo Duro and some on Frio Draw in a Capitol pasture, on which draw was the famous Mustang Lake. There was an excavation there but the lake seldom ever went dry.

"It was a very dry year on the Plains in 1887 when I worked in or with Frank Yearwood's cow outfit or wagon on the trail from Yellow Houses to the Canadian Breaks or Alamositas. They had about 30,000 head of cattle down on that end, mostly in the Yellow Houses and Sod House pastures and very little water—comparatively bad management by somebody—but we got them all out by December, 1887, but had a rough time doing it. We worked night and day at times and we suffered for water as well as the cattle and horses. Perry Cox, Waller, and Price and myself, others forgotten, were with the outfit from June 1 until we wound up with the last herd about December 15 at Sand Point Camp in an Escarbada pasture about twenty miles north of Escarbada headquarters in the Canadian Breaks. W. T. Kiens and Matt Larkin was with us that summer and all winter to June, 1885.

"When R. T. Bob Barton was discharged, most of his outfit went with him to the Bell Ranch over in New Mexico. That took place at Garcia Lake about eight miles northeast of Escarbada headquarters. It had a spring in the northeast corner of the Lake, or rather it was a larger depression in the Plains, and more of a valley than a lake, about a mile in diameter.

"But back to the ranches. I left Charleston, South Carolina, in the early part of 1885 and went to the World's Cotton Centennial at New Orleans and stayed there two weeks or more, then came on to Texas and landed in Abilene. I stayed there a short time, then went to the Spur Ranch and got a job as a cowboy. I had some learning to do, which I did fairly well in the next two years or more.

"Messrs. Loncep, Groff, Campbell, Stokes, and Davis were general managers, superintendent, wagon boss, and trail boss. They claimed 60,000 head of cattle, 615 saddle horses, and 414,000 acres of land and had it all fenced or practically closed with barbed wire in the fall of 1885. They counted all of the cattle they could find that year through a cross fence from the east to the west side of the pasture and only counted about 21,000 head. Then the Scotch part of the Company allowed them only 10 per cent on the range, count out sick or not yet found. Then they had sold 2,000 two-year-old Hereford that fall, 1885, to an Arizona outfit. Those Hereford were my first real stampede to participate in on Red Mud one night. I made a rep that night, or rather the horse did—and I got the credit. I was the first boy in the lead and turned the heads and thereby got them to milling and they were soon quiet. I may not have done so well but I could not hold him. So I done a reckless piece of riding that night over and through mesquite and won at the instigation of the horse and thereby got the praise of Stokes and Davis, wagon and trail bosses, and all for that matter was a prodigy of a greenhorn.

"But getting back to the cattle counting, the herd was said to be finally about 30,000. These had been cattle that had been taken range delivery when the Spur Company was formed about 1882 or 1883. We had a very hard winter there in 1884–1885, and the loss was heavy on the range. Mr. A. G. Boyce said in some instances it was as much as 60 per cent of the herd. The Spur also had many different brands, as they did not rebrand the cattle when they went into the company. I think they had about 115 different brands. They intended to get all the cattle in a few years with the Spur on them but the object of this count was to find out how many cattle they had as near as possible. The Scotch part of the company wanted to know, as it seems they bought a half interest in the company with a guarantee of 60,000 head of cattle and a dividend of 10 per cent of the sum; up to this time, 1885, it had paid only 3 per cent.

"So after this count they issued debentures on common stock to the American holders in half the original amount. So I think the Americans or old cowmen lost about all they had in it. . . .

"I had an escapade [on Spur Ranch] one night . . . with eight Apache young bucks and two girls or squaws, good looking and the chief supposed to be Geronimo. I was alone and did not feel very safe, but didn't act that way; so I had quite a pleasant time with them, especially with the two Indian girls—they seemed to take a liking to me. One of the Indians told me they would give me one of the girls if I wanted her. Of course I was not in a position to take her and excused myself the best I could.

"I had another experience there one night with a cougar. He got away, as I didn't have any gun that night, but he did get my horse, which he seemed to want. I had a gun on the night with the Apache Indians, but I didn't let them know it.

"When I left the Spur Company about June, 1887, I went

up to the Quaker colony Estancia on the Plains out about eighteen miles from Blanco Canyon and stayed that night with Mr. Dockeen. Before that he had been located down in the Spur Range in an early day and had a store and post office known as Dockeen's Ranch. . . . He was a New York man and had been a Union soldier. His wife was also a New York woman, very nice people. They also had a very nice and pretty daughter, Miss Grace Dockeen. I left my bed or some blankets with him, as I had a long ride to make that day and wanted to give my horse all the show possible. I went by Singer's Store on the Yellow Houses, where the city of Lubbock is now, I am told, and got dinner there and went on into a Yellow Houses pasture and stopped at a windmill and a tank about sundown eighteen miles from the Yellow Houses headquarters and stayed all night there and slept on my saddle blankets. I had a lunch and there was plenty of water there which was not the rule I found out later at many places in the XIT pastures at that time in 1887.

"I got to the Yellow Houses headquarters the next day before dinner. There I met the general manager, B. H. Campbell (Barbecue), and given a job at once with very few words and sent on to Earl Wright at the branding pen or corral nearby, where they were branding cattle, as they seemed convinced that I was pretty well versed in the old-time business.

"Mr. Boyce and Matlock came in a few days, which I knew at the time they would, as Mr. Campbell was leaving that day when he sent me to the branding pen, and I was not put on the payroll for a month after that, but, of course, it was all right, as Mr. Boyce and Matlock knew I was there. It's a reminder of the condition of things on the ranch when Mr. Boyce and Matlock took charge in June, 1887. Rollin Larrabee was bookkeeper at the time for the Yellow Houses for that end of the ranch. D. B. Braid and W. S. Mabry were the surveyors. Braid died in Tascosa about 1890. He was surveyor and a civil engineer. He was a fine young fellow. We had some association at times in connection with excavations, dams, etc. . . . he was about twenty-eight years of age when he died.

.   .   .   .

"Mr. Boyce got up an outfit with Frank Yearwood as wagon boss and of course I was in it. . . . in fact, we were all —Boyce and Matlock boys, except one or two, Billy Ney. The same old range boss went with us for a week or two also . . . went up to Spring Lake and in the meantime gathered up a heard of about 1200 four-year-old steers. . . . there were too many cattle on that end anyway. Something like 30,000 and water very short, which our outfit . . . put in the balance of the year 1887, getting them out and on up to a Rito Blanco pasture.

"In the meantime, Billy Ney and his one or two boys left us on Running Water Draw in Spring Lake, one morning after we had a stampede the night before. One of his boys went by the name of Arizona Johnny, somewhat on the 'bully' order. Of course our outfit didn't want any trouble, and didn't have any.

"We didn't lose any cattle that night, but Arizona Johnny got lost and stayed out all night. He didn't like it very much, . . . and wanted to put the blame for the stampede on the Boyce outfit. . . . I called him down, and he backed down. . . . It was a good thing he did, as there was some tension anyway. None of our boys said anything. . . . This was the last I ever saw of Billy Ney or Arizona Johnny. I think he went bad afterwards about 1888. . . .

"We had very little [good] influence if any thrown around us on the frontier and cow ranches in the eighties . . . until the XIT Ranch started a system of regeneration by putting the famous twenty-three rules into operation in 1888. . . .

[They] were fine rules morally and for a round of better conditions all over the ranch . . . , it did away gradually for XIT boys with Xmas Hell variety, this and gambling dens and anything that are compatible with them which led many good boys to destruction. . . .

"We on the XIT had a well drilled in 1892 about fourteen or fifteen miles north of Escarbada up the Mexico line in the Canadian Breaks that was a salt well. It was 405 feet deep. . . . I tested the well and . . . The water was very salty; when it settled, it left a coat of pretty white salt. . . . Wood tanks were done away with after 1887; they were too hard to keep up. Some were cemented, though, and they would crack with freezing.

"I remember when we were moving the cattle in 1887 out of the Yellow Houses and Spring Lake pastures; there was such a jam one time that we rounded up about 6,000 or thereabouts one day, all crazy for water. That night it took the whole outfit to hold them most of the time; the next night we were through the sand hills and into a Spring Lake pasture near the headquarters . . . on Black Water Draw. They still had no water. There is a soda lake about four miles west of Spring Lake headquarters which had water in it.

"They soon got the scent of it and the fun started again. The larger part of them went into it in spite of all we could do, except about eight hundred, which went toward the ranch, as there was a little water there and a larger corral. They went into the corral before they knew it, and we shut the gates; they were safe for the night, but the others not by any means. We had several situations like that that year, one in October similar on Black Water on the side of the pasture between Black Water and Running Water. It was cold and stormy that night. Waller Price, Shorty, and I were on first guard. We could not leave to wake the others up, as it took us both to hold them until just before day and the other guard could find us. The cook was up and cooking breakfast when I got the other guard. Though they were up they could not find us.

"I remember getting some bread out of an Indian grave on Running Water in a Spring Lake pasture one day in 1887. I thought at first I would take them, but after a little thought I put them back, as it seemed to be a sacrilege.

"Cowboys used to sing 'Pretty Little Girl I Left Far Behind' and 'The Little Old Sod Shanty on the Claim.' I am sure there were many Bobby Burns according to what there is now there in the eighties and nineties. Popular songs of the day were sung too."

C. H. Hanbury's duties had little concern with either cows or horses. Hanbury built things—chuck-wagon boxes, corrals, branding chutes, dipping vats, camp houses, and windmill towers. For thirty-three years he helped erect mills. When the syndicate wanted an edifice to house visiting customers and guests, he superintended construction of the Cold Water Hotel. When the turtles became a nuisance on Cheyenne Lake, Bob Duke asked Hanbury to build traps. At one time, so the story goes, more than two hundred turtles were taken from the traps.

Then came the wintry day of January 28, 1910:

"Mr. Duke and I left Channing, Texas, on the train for Perico or Farwell Park to build a new house. The old one had burned. We arrived there about nine o'clock that night. We slept in the barn loft; it was very cold. The next day, Bill Lytle, the windmiller, came in. He had his wagon and tent. The main wagon and the boys were burning fireguards on the state line. That day we put up his tent, and the ground was frozen so hard we couldn't drive pegs in the ground. So we had to tie the tent on locust trees. It was warmer sleeping on the frozen ground than it was in the barn loft. When the main wagon and the boys come, some of the boys worked on the house."

Arch Sneed's* account of working for the XIT could sound like the others—handling cattle, windmilling, riding line—except for his first winter of 1902–1903. By December of that year the cattle work was through, and the XIT had held its seasonal layoff of all except winter hands. Tobe Pitts gave the twenty-one–year–old Sneed an opportunity to stay on the payroll if he would freight salt, groceries, grain, and so on between such points as Perico, Buffalo Springs, Matlock, and Dalhart. He very quickly ran into trouble.

"I left Farwell Park with a load of grain for Matlock Camp, where they kept two men, R. E. Tribble and S. K. Coates. They each had four saddle horses and I had a load of grain for their camp. It was daylight when I left Farwell Park on February 21, 1903. The ground was covered with snow and it was snowing hard, but not blowing. It is about twenty-five miles from Farwell Park to Matlock Camp. I had

---

* Most of the cowboys leaving reminiscences failed to tell how they happened to seek ranching as a livelihood. Arch Sneed is an exception, with a rather vivid account that shows easily how a boy's imagination could be fired:

"I was born in Lampasas County [Texas], June 13, 1881. In the north end of the county was what was known as the Old Beef Trail, and ran right by my house. It was near a spring known as Beef Pen Spring. When I was a small boy, my sister and I use to watch the big trail herds of cattle from the coast going north, and it seemed to me they would pass for hours. We were watching through the cracks of a ten-rail fence. These steers were from four to ten years old, coaster steers, big longhorns out of the brush. The men wore leather chaps and toe fenders over the stirrups and all of them carried rifles and pistols. Many of them carried them across the pommel of their saddle and not in a scabbard as we do today.

"That was when I first got my idea that I want to be a cowboy."

a four-horse team and 6,000 pounds of grain. Before I had gone ten miles the road was covered up in the short-grass country until I could see no place of the road, but I managed to stay on it until I got into the sand hills, where the tall grass made the road visible. That being my first big snowstorm in the Panhandle, I had a horror of being lost with that team, but I stayed on the road until I reached Matlock Camp. There was no other road from Farwell Park to Matlock Camp. When I reached the camp, I met John Godfrey, who had come from Buffalo Springs with a four-horse load of hay. He had the same experience I had about finding the road on account of the snow, which by that time was getting very deep.

"Next morning, the twenty-second, the snow was sure deep and was still snowing; so we didn't attempt to move. The storm lasted three days and nights, the twenty-first, twenty-second, and twenty-third. We four men were in that dugout, which was completely covered up with snow, but we would dig our way out to feed and care for sixteen head of horses which we had there. The cows and calves were drifting along the fence, bawling and dying in piles. These cattle were the first cows and calves at Buffalo Springs, it formerly having been a steer division, and they had been driven from Alamositas Pasture, which is now the Matador Ranch—they had sold this ranch to the Matadors—and moved these cattle to Buffalo Springs. These cattle had been accustomed to breaks or rough country, where they had been protected, and the severity of the storm told on them. There were cows and calves dying and bawling all along the dugout and against the fence. The storm broke the twenty-third, and the weather was pretty from then on; we had no more bad weather that winter but there was snow on the ground yet May first in drifts and shady places. We couldn't move our freight teams or anything; so we started in to help skin cattle. Tobe Pitts,

Fidel Trujillo, and Walter Williams came from Buffalo
Springs to Matlock Camp after the storm had broken and we
all started in skinning cattle. I don't know how many cattle
they lost in this storm, but there was dead cattle piled against
the fence all the way from where Kofer's dairy is now to
Texline by Ware, that fence across the Fort Worth and Denver at Ware. There were many dead antelope against the
fence which had drifted with the cattle and died.

"I had been in Dallam County continuously since that
time and made it my home, but have never seen a storm as
severe or as much snow as we had that spell. I think Andy
James will verify that fact. Andy had cattle up there at that
time. The only cows we could skin were the ones yet with cir-
culation. They were down and couldn't get up. We would cut
their throats and skin them while yet warm. The ones which
had been dead for some time were frozen so hard that we
couldn't possibly skin them."

Blue Stevens had a brief turn at freighting also, once driving a six-mule team to Amarillo for supplies:

"The boss told me to put four mules to the wagon to load,
and I made a mistake and put the swing mules for leaders.
We did fine until we got to the wagon yard. The gate got in
our way; so we took it off, a little ragged like, but it was clean
gone when we got through. The old man ran in the house,
scared we would get the house next, I guess. It cost just about
fifty dollars straightening up the damage me and the mules
did. My loss was small, just a few toenails, during the excitement."

The incident marked the end of Blue Stevens as a freighter, which probably pleased him.

Part of the job on the XIT, if a man was of legal age, consisted of doing his duty for the ranch's interests whenever
politics came around. Isolated as they were, the hands had
little concern about what went on in the state or national po-

litical arenas, but what happened in Dallam or Sherman or any of the other eight counties into which the XIT intruded was a vital matter. Or to put it the other way, Bill Armstrong writes of an important suit that arose, but at once dismisses it with these words: "We did not understand it; it was not on the ranch."

There was no such thing as a political party in the area. Nor were the sides selected on a progressive-conservative line, or cattleman against farmer. Usually the contenders were the candidates put up by the XIT against the candidates representing the neighboring LS Ranch. Whoever won, the cattle interests prevailed.*

One feature was dependable—the man elected remained close to his electorate. When Perry Cox celebrated his victory to public office by getting "a little tipsy," he was forced to resign, according to Blue Stevens. Ira Aten's bossing duties included overseeing a pasture which in turn included one half of Deaf Smith County. For eight years Aten was elected and re-elected county commissioner for that half, which he would have had to look after anyhow, in his XIT capacity, and for those eight years he had the support of a solid bloc of twenty cowboys who constituted a majority of the eligible voters. In some counties getting elected was not quite so easy. Tobe Pitts had to offer to resign from his XIT position to get elected treasurer of Dallam County. And another hand was elected assessor, so it was claimed, only because he was the father of several pretty daughters (all girls were pretty in that woman-scarce country) and most cowboys were single and interested.**

---

* Arch Sneed swears that he was turned down the first time he applied to the XIT for a job because he was under twenty-one: ". . . they wanted to work men that were old enough to vote so they could have a say-so in politics."

** Letter from J. S. Kenyon.

Fred Graven became involved in Panhandle politics because he had attended academy before coming west and could spell. He found Sherman County,* where he was first stationed, a hotbed of politics, with cowboys from all over the area coming into Sherman to cast votes for one side or the other "or maybe both sides if they could get away with it." The only difference that Graven could see in the contending parties was that one was in office and the other wanted in.

"The population all told of men, women, and children to the last baby would make maybe fifty. Of course the women and children were not included in the politics. Both sides went over into Oklahoma and got votes. It was a game of wits as to who would come out ahead.

" 'Now Loomis has never taken any side in the elections that they have over there,' said George Westmoreland, 'and he hasn't the time to make out election reports and so on, to be sent to Austin, and they won't trust anybody else to make reports. Most of them couldn't make a report if they had to do so. You are not old enough to vote or they would be after your vote in the next election. Besides, you will make a little money, more than I am paying you as a cowboy, and further,' he went on, 'I always want to get along with my neighbors if at all possible.'

"So I went back with Fred Loomis. I stayed with his father and mother. They had two or three extra rooms, as they had the only hotel. Fred Loomis had told me that there were about fifty people in the county, not enough to do the county work, but we sure reported that many voters in the county."

Extreme care had to be taken, it might be added, in making out election returns to certify to the state government in Austin. A bit of carelessness and you might wind up with more votes than you had people.

* Sherman County adjoins Dallam County to the east.

The length to which one outfit would go to keep its competitor from winning is shown by Allen Stagg:

"With reference to elections, I recall that at the election the fall of 1900 I was working for the LS Ranch but as I had filed on some land in an LE pasture, I had to vote at Bravo, as well as Jess Morris, who also had some land in the LE. Bob was working for the election of Pete Frederick as against Henry McGee for sheriff, and Bob had made arrangements for some six or eight settlers who lived south of an Alamositas pasture to come to his camp the day before election and he would pilot them to Bravo to vote. Jess and I did not know of this until we got to Alamositas. As we did not want to make the long ride from Tascosa to Bravo in one day, we did not get to Alamositas until after dark. So our horses did not get with the rest of the horses in the pastures.

"Next morning Bob got up early and all the horses were gone except mine and Jess's. I loaned him mine and he found that they had all been driven off to the South Plains, and he could not find them. However, he found a bunch of locoed horses and brought them and with the work mules mounted all the men there. Jess and I rode our own horses. We left some of the locoed horses and I went on ahead and told Gene Elliston what had happened, and he sent a wagon out to meet the bunch and took them to Bravo. I could see that the whole bunch, including Bob, thought I had something to do with it, as they supposed we would vote for McGee, but neither of us did.

"I never knew who did this until several years later, I was riding with Lem Eaves, an LS cowboy and he asked me who I thought did that. I told him that I did not have any idea, but that everybody else thought that I did it. 'Well,' he said, 'I know you didn't do it, for I did it myself. I thought I would set you fellows afoot because I knew every one of you would vote for Pete.' Then he told me who was there, as he looked through the window and saw us all. He took the horses clear out of the pasture south of the gate and turned them loose in the 'strip.' But he missed the mules and Jess's and my horse.

"He said that the LS bosses did not know who did it and never had suspected him; neither did Harry McGee know it."

And so one after another the accounts run. These were the proud men on horseback, riding the range of the nation's largest spread, roping and trailing, and disdainful of men who had to walk their way through life. But they were men, too, who sometimes had to walk, to crawl, to put up fences and take down fences, to mow hay, to doctor sick cows, to lay in a winter crop. They were, after all, working men; and though the chores sketched briefly here were humdrum at best and often downright disagreeable, they were nonetheless necessary. And the cowboy was a hired hand, employed to do whatever had to be done about a ranch.

On the other hand, life on the XIT was not entirely lacking in adventure and imaginative appeal. The writers of Western novels and scenarios do have some touch with reality, as some of the following chapters will show.

FIRE FIGHTING

THE PANHANDLE of Texas has never been no-
torious for excessive rainfall, except for an occasional gully-
washer that makes a temporarily demoniacal torrent out of
such usually placid rivers as the Canadian. But for days on
end, and sometimes even for weeks and months, the rain can
refuse to fall and the clouds fail to gather. Meanwhile a light
wind, behaving for all the world like an unceasing soft sand-
blast, whips across the High Plains, searing whatever growth
and topsoil the sun hasn't already baked.

One result of this incessant thermal activity is that a fire on
a Panhandle spread is an epic production, fueled by the
strawlike quality of the grass and whipped by the breeze into

a beauteous, fearsome, encompassing thing. Thus a harmless XIT grass fire might almost literally explode into a holocaust that consumes thousands of acres of pasturage, as well as anything human, animal, or man-erected that had once stood on those now burnt-over acres. The loss in assets might prove cataclysmic; the danger to the living just might eclipse the suffering of the pocketbook.

To obviate such disaster cowboys were regularly detailed to plow fireguards. It was mean, back-breaking work, fit only for farmers, but the cowboys went ahead carving out their fire brakes and holding their grumbling to a minimum because they knew that they were buying insurance—insurance against a halfway innocuous prairie fire that might involve them in a killing contest before it had spent itself.* It is no wonder that when the XIT hands set themselves down to write their reminiscences so many of them gave a lion's share of the space to a fire they had experienced.

"A great fire had broke out on this side of the Pecos River in New Mexico," writes Gene Elliston. "A high wind from the west was blowing and continued to blow for several days. Of course the fire swept east over the staked plains. There was no streams or anything to check it until it reached the Texas line. There the XIT outfit had a fireguard seventy-five feet wide plowed and burned out. However, the wind was so high and the cow chips was [so] dry it would blow the fiery chips across the guard. It was then in Texas on the XIT range. The fire went almost to Amarillo. It burned thousands and thousands of acres of grass. Of course there was some draws like Tierra Blanca and others that now are washed out that would probably turn some fire, but then,

* Ira Aten, who had things he would rather be about, estimates that he plowed 150 miles of fireguards in one summer. This was done, of course, before the days of tractors, and was accomplished with turning plows and sulkeys, or gang plows hitched to mules.

these same draws, the bottoms of them was a mat of grass, so the fire swept on, until the wind finely went down, the fire died out. Mack Huffman was foreman at the Spring Lake Division of the XIT.

"The wind was blowing strong from the north; we could see a long way north as we were yet in a high elevation. All of a sudden the smoke began boiling up in the XIT Middle Water Pasture about fifty miles away. Colonel Boyce scratched his head, looked at our boss and said, 'Montgomery, if that fire is not out when you get this herd into Rito Blanco Pasture you catch the best horses you have, take your men, and go to it.' Said he, 'We have lost a big part of our south range and we can't afford to lose the north part.'

"Right then my whiskers growed an inch. I said, 'Colonel less order a snow.' He said, 'You go to that herd.' And I went. We began to move them, and about three o'clock in the evening the wind was still blowing a gale from the north."

In this instance Elliston and his companions were rescued by that snow he suggested the Colonel order. Needless to say, not all fires were handled this felicitously. Bob Beverly's experience, for instance, was considerably more trying. Writes Beverly:

"As Dick Estes and I came back from a two-days' drunk, at Clayton, in the spring of 1894, Dick would strike matches to light his cigarette, and kept throwing the match down in the dry grass, and I told him he was going to burn the grass off. He said he would make a lot of work for the hands of the ranch, as they was too stingy to go up to Clayton and spend their money.

"About the time we reached the northwest corner of Texas, and was loping along down the XIT fence, going east to the ranch, I looked back and all the country southeast of the Rabbit Ear Mountains was covered with smoke. As the wind was from the northwest, getting stronger and stronger, it was coming toward the XIT Pasture, about as fast as a man could ride horseback. About the time we had drank our last drink, and stopped to take a look at the country we had come over, I saw the ranch boys coming horseback, and behind them a hack with a barrel of water and loaded down with feed sacks, brooms, etc.

"I knew then that we should get to come back the way we had come and we did; but the fire jumped the fireguard between the northwest corner of Texas and Texline. The next morning I gave out and lay down about ten miles north of where Ware is now; the fire looked to me to be about north of where Dalhart is now.

"When I woke up it was about three o'clock the second day, and about night it went to raining, and I just allowed myself to lay down on my saddle blanket, and take an all-night rain. I finally found Dick Estes and asked him what he thought of the work that he had started. He said it was O.K. as the country needed burning off. He was a great Irishman."

The most damaging fire of all seems to have been a three-day affair that several cowboys write about. J. W. Armstrong's account is the fullest:

"I have been in many fires, the largest being of seventy-two hours' duration, and as far as I know the largest in the Ranch's history. Fires were of great extent and damage, grass being dense and nothing to break the sweep of the raging flames. Orders were to go to any fires within a radius of a hundred miles. Sacks, saddle blankets, brooms, or chaps were used to fight fires with till you got men and horses enough to kill a cow, split her open and turn the flesh side down and drag her on the edge of the fire line, and if you had horses enough you kill two of the cows and tie them together side by side so as to cover a wider space and drag the two of them, sixteen or twenty head of horses being required for this dragging the cows by the horn of the saddles. They soon exhaust the horses because of the rapid speed of the fire, horses often have to go in a lope. However the smoke exhausts the horse perhaps quicker, because a horse cannot stand smoke. Therefore a horse has to be changed every half mile to a mile. The heavier the cow a better job, hence often a bull is slaughtered instead of a cow, this is if there are horses enough to drag the animals. You could put out more fire in this manner than fifty men could with sacks and blanket fighting. When the flesh of the cows were charred from the fire they were drug aside and another slaughtered to take their place.

"Men were placed in relays every hundred yards, to fight out the little spots of fire left after the drag had gone by. These men had to go in a run to keep up; therefore a new man was dropped out every hundred yards for this purpose, leaving his horse where he started for the man fighting fire to pick up and bring back to the main fire and there to drop out again when his turn came. Every man riding his own horse and taking time about, dragging the cows, dropping out again to hand-fight the remaining spots of fire, when his time came.

"Eating, of course, was out of the question as long as the fire raged. In the seventy-two—hour fire mentioned we became so exhausted after forty-eight hours of fighting that food was provided. This fire started in the 101 Pasture south of where Dalhart is located and came into Middle Water Pasture about two miles north of where Middle Water is now, crossing the Middle Water Pasture to the New Mexico line, burning all the grass off the north half of the Middle Water Division. Fire was still raging when a new fire came in from the southwest from New Mexico. This fire burned south of Middle Water Creek and between Middle Water Creek and the main draw. This fire was fought by the ST, and another XIT cowboy and I helped this outfit fight the fire. The ST Ranch was located on Ute Creek in New Mexico. During the fighting of the fire (XIT) the boys having reached the old freight road, Middle Water and Farwell Park road, the exhausted boys refused to fight any further till they got something to eat, laying down in this freight wash till I went about fifteen miles to Middle Water Ranch for food for them, all the horses having been exhausted but mine and my brother John's horse.

"When I got to the ranch R. C. Clendennin, the windmiller, was already loading prepared food into the windmill wagon to bring to the boys. By the time we got back out there the boys' tongues had swollen so that they could eat only oatmeal and some couldn't even eat that. This was on the twenty-first day of March, 1895. We left this spot about 4 P.M. and it was eight miles from the New Mexico line. Before we got through the wind turned straight to the west and another fire started in south of Clayton and burned off all the grass from the south side of the tracks of the Fort Worth and Denver to the edge of where the fire had burned. In there grass was six feet south of Ware, and cattle had drifted ahead of the fire till they reached the XIT fence. There 750 of them were burned to death. Then the wind changed to the north and it snowed and the wind blew so hard it blew the fire out. That was the first time I ever knew a wind to get so high it put out a fire."

A year earlier Ira Aten participated in a fire that spread over three counties. It started immediately after a cow outfit struck camp just west of the Pecos River near Fort Sumner, New Mexico.

"The cook allowed the camp fire to get away from him and it started up a draw where the outfit was camped. Then it headed east for the Plains country, helped by a wind blowing fifty miles an hour from the west. There had been heavy rains during the summer and the grass had grown luxuriantly.

"Ranchers and settlers at that time had very few fireguards. During the winter season the wind was nearly always from the west, blowing at a fifty- to sixty-mile clip. Of course this made it difficult to stop prairie fires.

"This time the wind blew a regular hurricane for three days and nights and the fire swept through the eastern part of New Mexico, into western Texas, ravaging Parmer, Castro, and Swisher counties as far as Amarillo and Plainview Road. This road was used as a cattle trail to Amarillo shipping point, and no grass grew for a quarter mile on each side of it.

"The north half of Bailey, Lamb, and Hale counties, as well as the south half of Deaf Smith and Randall counties, were also in the line of the fire. This region was just being settled by 'nesters,' as they were called. Some few settlers had fireguards plowed and burned over and thus saved some grass, while others lost everything they possessed.

"Many cattle and antelope caught in the lead fire and hemmed in fence corners were burned to death. Cattle can run through a side fire without any bad effect except the hair being somewhat singed. Not so with the lead fire, as it is like an inferno.

"The plains grass called 'grama' or 'buffalo' grass does not grow tall like the Kansas sage grass, and fire does not travel as fast. Ten or twelve miles an hour is about as fast as the plains grass fire traveled even in a high wind. The lead fire in a strong wind will whip around and check its speed and would almost stop at times like in a whirlwind. The large lakes on the plains would stop a lead fire for a time and it may be an hour before it got around the lake and got the lead fire started again. We at Dimmitt saw the smoke of this fire for two days before it got to Dimmitt and was backfiring against it on every trail and road before it got there.

"Next summer everybody went to plowing fireguards.

"A good fireguard is six furrows wide (with a twelve-inch

plow) on both sides of a two-hundred-foot space which is left to be burned off in the fall just as soon as the grass is dry enough. As a general rule a fireguard two hundred feet wide is enough to stop a fire, although I have known cases in which flames driven by a fifty- or sixty-mile gale would jump across a two-hundred-foot guard.*

"Definite instructions were given to all the men to quit their work and hurry to any place on the ranch where a fire had broken out. When this happened, the nearest camp man come with a light wagon, on which all the grub at hand would be loaded: coffee and coffee pot, a barrel of water, and six heavy brooms. These brooms were kept at each camp and were used to follow the drag and sweep out the little sparks which the drag might have passed over.

"A fire drag in the early days consisted of a yearling which was cut in half. The hide was taken off one half and allowed to drag behind to act as a smother for the sparks missed by the beef half. Here's how the drag was used: After cutting off the head the fleshy part of the animal was laid on the ground, flesh part down. One rope was tied to the forefoot and another to the hind foot of the carcass, the ropes tied to

* Charley Alford, who is still going strong in Amarillo as this is written, says that fireguards were always plowed during the busy branding time. "Three men were sent out, two to plow and one to cook. They plowed these guards around the entire ranch on the outside of the entire border of the ranch.

"Two furrows were plowed, most of the time in September, and then about the middle of November and through December 10 or 12 would burn these guards. Three men with ropes soaked in coal oil with several men following with brooms, so if the fire jumped the guard they would be there to put it out.

"If it was wet or windy we would have to lay up and wait until the grass dried enough to burn and wind to quit blowing. We would burn at night lots of times until twelve o'clock or later.

"Then another big furrow was plowed during this burning."

the saddle horns of two horses. One horse would go over the burned stubble, the other on the grass, the beef dragging over the fire line.

"A horse could not stand walking over the burned stubble more than a half hour at a time without being relieved, as the ground would be so hot it would ruin his feet. Several of our horses were injured in that manner and it took just a year for their hoofs to grow off and then they would be all right again. Whenever we had a horse burned in that way we turned him loose in the Canadian Breaks horse pasture and forgot about him for one year.

"It is to be understood that there are two fire lines for every fire and the same process would be gone through on each fire line. It took two yearlings for each fire and five men to each drag to do good fast work. Two men were needed to pull the beef drag by the horns of their saddles. Two men handled the brooms and if brooms were not available they used their saddle blankets. One of the men followed close behind the drag, generally in a trot to keep up with the drag, the other was a hundred yards back to kick in the smoking cow chips from the grass line. The fifth man would stay on his horse, a quarter of a mile or more behind the others, looking for backfire from neglected burning cow chips in the line. The backfire was very important to watch and one soon learned that lesson when he had to turn around and retrace his course several miles to do his work all over again.

"It made a man sick to see a fire starting up behind him a mile or two.

"Ten men were required to fight a fire systematically—a big, big fire, such as we had to battle so often in the early days of the plains.

"Later I had chain drags made, which were something like a fish net, six by eight feet with meshes six inches square.

"One of these chain drags was kept at each camp. A barrel

of water was always ready with two large hides in it to put over the chain drag to smother the flames, and this arrangement prove[d] much better than the beef drag.

"In this way we kept the damages from prairie fires on the ranch at a minimum. When the fire broke out some of the men might be in a few miles of the danger spot while others would be thirty miles away. The first men to arrive on the scene would kill the beef and make everything ready and by that time there would be enough men on hand to go down the most dangerous fire line. Later arrivals would take the other fire line, and you see about twelve or fifteen men were sometimes on the job in a fire-fighting crew.

"I will long remember a day in December, 1895. I had just arrived at ranch headquarters a few hours before, when a ranchman ran in and said there was a big fire to the north. The headquarters men had been given positive instructions to go up on a high windmill tower and keep a lookout for fire whenever a strong wind was blowing and the grass was dry enough to burn. This man had spotted a fire from his lookout post on the tower.

"I took a good look at the fire and judged that it was near the head of the Mojares Canyon, about thirty miles away on the plains. I mounted my best horse immediately and started, at a slow gallop for the first five miles, checking my horse occasionally to a walk or a trot, so he could get his breath and warm up slowly. After that I turned him loose. When I got to the scene of the blaze many of the boys were there. They were going down each line of fire with their beef drags in good order. They knew they could count on my arrival as soon as my horse could take me to the fire. I never failed to go to a fire, although sometimes the men had the blaze well under control by the time I got there.

"This day the wind was blowing very strong from the west, as usual at that season of the year. A fire is much easier to drag out in a strong wind, because then there is no zig-zag in the fire line.

"We dragged the fire out to our east line of fence, some fifteen miles, and then it went out in the strip country, where men were waiting, and the fire fighting was taken up by them, from there on. We finished our work about nine o'clock at night and rode ten miles to Tombstone Camp, which was the nearest camp, and we were glad to get there for the night. After questioning the boys closely as to the origin of this fire and finding that none of the men had been near the place where it first started, I decided I would investigate further the following day.

"I rode the New Mexico fence line along the Endee country and found a place that showed tracks of two men and horses coming through the fence going east. The tracks showed that one horse had been shod all around with heels and toes, while the other was shod only on the front feet with smooth shoes. I also noticed a peculiarity in the tracks— that there were only three nails on the right hind shoe on the first horse. I felt I had enough information to recognize these tracks if I ever saw them again, and I decided to go over to Endee, about five miles in New Mexico, to find out who had left there for Texas the day before.

"As a result of my inquiries there I found that a well-known wild mustang catcher and tamer had left Endee with a boy the day before, headed for the strip country in Texas east of the XIT Ranch, where this man had a small bunch of cattle and some horses. This man had asked permission a few months before to catch some wild mustangs in one of my pastures and I had refused. Because of the information I got, I became just a little suspicious of this fellow.

"I had decided to stay at the Trujillo Camp for the night on the New Mexico fence line about ten miles from Endee.

As I was jogging along the road toward camp I saw two men coming down the road toward me. Suddenly they whirled their horses off the road and went at great speed down a draw. I recognized them as the two men I had been told had left Endee for Texas the day before, and my suspicions were strengthened.

"I got off my horse and examined the tracks in the road and the marks of their horses' hoofs were exactly the same as the tracks I had found going through the fence. It was getting too dark to make out the number of nails in the shoe prints, but I felt sure they were the men who had set the fire the day before.

"I could not make up my mind what to do, and continued my way to camp in a slow trot with my head down, just thinking—thinking what was best to do. If they set fire to our pastures once they would do it again. If I accused them of it, it would make them angry and then they surely would burn me out. I could not study out any plan of action to pursue.

"I must have ridden several miles absorbed in thought, and when I looked up the heavens seemed all ablaze ten miles ahead of me. As nearly as I could tell the fire was in my winter bull pasture, under the breaks, a three-league pasture. I put spurs to my horse and only thought of getting to the fire, but my suspicions run high that the same two men had come back through the breaks and set my bull pasture on fire. I did not use this pasture in the summertime, but kept the bulls there when I gathered them in December for winter pasture.

"My mind was taken up with thoughts of getting to the fire so that I quit thinking about the suspects and spurred on all the faster. When I got to the fire a few of the boys were there, fighting for dear life. Other men kept come[ing] until most of the ranch hands were there. We could not use a fire drag. The grass was heavy bunch grass. We had to use our wet saddle blankets and heavy brooms to whip out the fire.

"We fought that fire all night long, and just at sunup the last spark was put out. There was no wind blowing; so the fire burned slowly in every direction.

"Some of the boys fell in their tracks, they were so dead tired and sleepy, having fought the fire the night before.

"The sun came up bright and warm on that December morning. It was more than a half hour before I could arouse the men to get up and go to the nearest camp at Trujillo to get something to eat. Some of the men had had no dinner and none had supper the day before.

"We slept all day at the camp and late in the evening I got up and rode to ranch headquarters, thirty miles to the south. After a good sleep and rest that night my mind began to work on the suspects again. Putting all the facts together and studying them carefully, I knew who had set those two fires just the same as if I had seen them in the act. My mind was quickly made up. I would put the fear of death into their hearts, just as the government is doing today in kidnap cases.

"It was common talk among the cattle rustlers in the Endee country 'burn them out and he will not be able to hold his job.'

"I got my most trusted horse and started out carrying my light saddle gun and six-shooter with me. For a month I dropped at camps and ranches in Texas and New Mexico where this man would be most likely to hang out. I waylaid the trail he was in the habit of crossing the ranch. I was determined that the country was not large enough to hold him and me, too. If he stayed in the country I was sure we would meet some day and then there would be a reckoning. I gave little thought to the boy. I felt that he did not know what kind of fire he was playing with.

"This man kept just two jumps ahead of me. I did not ask any questions about him. I just looked and listened. Suspecting that I was hunting for him, his friends advised him to leave the country.

"He sold his little bunch of cattle and horses for what he could get and went to Cripple Creek, Colorado.

"I never heard of his being in Texas any more until after I had left the ranch for California. I thank God I never saw him again. I understand that he did return to his old haunts eventually and died a natural death."

Several of the men tell of a fire started by a spark from a Fort Worth and Denver locomotive that spread from Matlock to the Cimarron River. Charlie Alford was on his way to fight it, when he "ran across a well-driller's camp built on a wagon set out in high grass. The driller was gone but wife and two children were there. I burned a back fire all around the camp and saved her and the children."

Not all fires left calamity in their wake. J. A. Smiley tells of one in which still another cook let the fire get out of control. "Some of our bedding got burned nearly up," recalls Smiley, "and one wagon wheel liked to have burned down. Old Lan [the cook] finally got the fire out around the wagon after he had wasted his barrel of water fighting it with a wet sack, he was just about all in when we got to the wagon."

One other account should be included here, not because the fire was of any consequence but because of the artfulness with which L. L. Derrick describes it:

"George Findlay put me to riding the range and talleying the dead cattle. I road from Yellow Houses north and I got 874 carcasses, 81 at one well. I think it was the fourteenth of January they was a preary fire came in from southwest in that Coyote Lake country. I had left camp early and had gone eight or ten miles before I saw the fire; so I turned for camp.

They were a hay-baling outfit there baling hay; so when I got to camp the boss, Taylor was his name, got to the fire about ten o'clock.

"Frank Yearwood, Oscar Cordill, and a nigger, Jo Johnson, and the hayin' boys was fightin' the fire. We finely put it out on the east and north and went to the west side. Perry Cox and Felix Castelo, that was camped at Black Water, came to us, and Yearwood sent them to watch the north side and the fire didn't break out again, as that was clost to XIT fence. The wind was from southwest, and about midnight it changed to northeast. I told the boys the wind changed; so some of them didn't think so; so pretty soon it commenced showerin'; so the fire went out."

Two facts concerning the fighting of prairie fires that all the XIT hands seem to agree on are that everyone pitched in to put out a fire, whether it was on his property or not, and that fighting was hard work and made a hand hungrier than almost any other activity. Says Charles Burrus: "Neighbor ranchmen always came to help fight fires." And J. W. Standifer tells how a group he was with on the Punta de Agua spotted a fire a good twenty-five miles away on a cold day. Despite the fact that the cowboys were near their home camp and had no food for a journey, they struck out, so "hungry we could have eaten anything." They did, in fact, lick the cold tallow from the Dutch oven that was in one of their wagons. It took the men twelve hours to reach the fire, which was extinguished by then, and another twelve hours to get home.

"But that was the custom of the country, everybody dropped everything that they were doing and went to fight fire."

But despite their willingness to do whatever would help to diminish damage from fires, most cowboys would agree with

Standifer when he admits that "I guess this and haying was the hardest work we did, or it was what we hated worse anyway." A prairie fire might be spectacular and even a thing of beauty, but to the cowboy it was an enemy—hated, hateful, dreaded, and to be destroyed at whatever the cost in weary muscles, smarting eyes, lank bellies, or singed hides.

HERDING

THE BUGGY CREAKED ALONG over the rolling prairie that to the eye looked as smooth as an ironing board but that to the seat felt like one durned cliff after another. Mack Huffman was driving. As they topped a rise, Huffman's companion stood up suddenly in the buggy and took a long look.

"I knew the X's had lots of country but I didn't know they had this much," he observed.

"Sit down, John," said Huffman, "I'm not half done showing you yet."

Many a man came to work for the XIT without, like Huffman's friend, seeing half of the ranch. But one thing all

hands had in common, whether they worked on one of the
lower ranches, or on one of the upper ones, or on the topping-
off spread in Montana—they all at some time herded cattle,
frequently from one division to another, so that in these
reminiscences they give more space to their jobs as wardens
for a bunch of disinterested steers than to any other phase
of their XIT activity. And no matter how joyous or how
necessary other tasks might seem, looking to the cattle always came first.

When Thanksgiving Day, 1894, came around, for instance, cowboys from Amarillo to Trinidad converged on
Channing for a dance. While they were swinging the girls
high and stomping the floor hard, word came that a fire had
burned off most of the Spring Lake Division, scattering the
cattle and necessitating their being herded north to Rito
Blanco. Unhappily, but without hesitancy, the hands dropped
their partners, put away their drinks, and started out into
the chill of late autumn. Gene Elliston tells the story:

"We had to take two wagons, chuck wagon and grain
wagon, as we had to feed our horses grain, as the grass was
all burned up. We had five horses to the man. There was
eight cowboys and wrangler, that means one man that took
care of the horses, nine riders and two wagon men, including
cook.

"I set in the saddle astride a horse in the Panhandle near
twenty-four years, and I will state right here this was the
toughest job I ever saw. It was as fine a bunch of men that
ever went with a cow wagon. It took true metal to stay on
this job. The weather was cold. We camped on the north
side of the burn one night, we traveled all the next day going
south and finely camped. We were not yet to the south side
of the burn, but was as far south as we need take our wagons.
So Mack Huffman sent us a man that night to stay with us
so that he could lead the drive next morning as we did not

know the country and did not know just how Mack Huffman
wanted us to get the cattle. We had to stand guard around
our horses, as there was no grass, just bedded them down
and watched to see that they did not stray and had to feed
them corn which one of the wagons hauled.

"Well, next morning by the crack of daylight we were in
the saddle going south in a fast run to the south line of the
Capitol Pasture. There we began to find cattle. These cattle
had not anything to eat for ten days; lots of cows had quit
their calves. Mack Huffman sent a man by the name of Joe
Anderson to lead the drive; a finer cowboy never rode a
horse.

"Well, we throwed the cattle together, five thousand head,
big calves, little calves, cows, bull stags, everything in the
cow line that could walk. Here is where the fun commenced.
In my imagination now, I sometimes think I can still hear
those cattle bawling. There was just cattle and mustangs left
in the country, as the antelopes had drifted ahead of the fire
and crawled through the fences, got out of the way.

"We headed north with our herd. We stood guard with
our overshoes, caps, and overcoats on—in fact we had to
wear these clothes all the time, night and day, the weather
being so cold. We had eight cowboys, stood four men to the
guard, guard half of the night each. We sure had something
to do. At times it looked as though we could not hold the
cattle.

"The second day at noon we got off the burn country,
watered at Tombstone Camp. The cattle were so crazy they
would not graze and fill up as usual; so we cowboys had to
be on the alert every second to hold them. We throwed the
herd out of the XIT pasture at Tombstone Camp just east
of the camp.

"There were two men staying in the camp, one by the
name of Tom Sheens, the other I don't remember his name,

but I remember how Tom Sheens laughed and joshed us boys
at having such a tough job, said he sure enjoyed seeing us
boys having to work a little. We were eating supper, that is,
the relief was, and I was on herd. Tom Sheens was with me
riding around cocked over on one side of his horse laughing
and having lots of fun out of me when Colonel Boyce drove
up in his buggy.

"He looked the herd over, then turned to the boss and
said, 'You had best throw this herd into Alamositas Pasture
before daylight.' And it was fifteen miles away. He then
turned to Tom Sheens and said, 'You and your man go with
them.' Then it was our time to laugh at Tom, and we sure
did a good job of it.

"After we got through eating supper we caught fresh
horses, the best ones we had, and started the cattle. As the
old saying is, the night was clear as a bell and as cold as
H——. A man by the name of Rainyway and myself was
pointers. That means that he and I was to hold the lead cattle straight, as we knew the country and where we were going. Along about eleven o'clock the swing man come up,
that is the man working behind Rainey and I. He told us the
boss said to hold up the lead cattle; so we did, and at this
particular spot it chanced to be an old bed ground and there
was plenty of cow chips.

"We soon had about two thousand head of the cattle bedded down. We asked the swing man how far back it was to
the drags. He said he went back until he met the flank man
and the flank man said he had been back as far as five miles
and met the boss. He told him that the drags was so far back
he could not hear their bawl; so you see we were then covering a good deal of territory. So there was not much left for
Rainey and I to do; so we soon gathered a big lot of cow
chips and built a big fire to keep from freezing.

"We told each other of all the hairbreadth escapes we had

had. We had begun to get a trifle drowsy, when all of a sudden a great commotion come over the hine end of the herd; the lead cattle started to running, we jumped in our saddles and went with them. Finely we got our end of the herd settled down; the swing man came up.

"I ask him, 'For God's sake! What had happened to the drags?'

"He said, 'That dam fool Tom Sheens and Bull S—— Bob Fields!' They had found an old carcass of a cow that had died the winter before and her bones was yet in the hide, so one tied his rope to the tail, the other to her head, then tied the ropes to the horns of their saddles. They would ride far enough apart and pull the ropes tight. They would reach out with their hands, get hold of the ropes and jerk the old carcass off the ground, then let it back with a thump, and the bones rattling in that hide, you can imagine what was happening.

"Well, they did not pull this many times until Bob's horse throwed him off; so Sheens had to cut the rope at the horn of his saddle. That turned Bob's horse loose with the carcass tied to him. Bucking was too slow for him then; so he began to run right through the herd. Of course he did not run far until he run over a cow and fell down. He got up with the rope under his tail; so he taken a fresh start, but he did not go far until he run over another cow and fell again. So when he got up this time the saddle had turned and he broke the rope.

"There is something peculiar about a horse. Always when a broke horse gets in distress he will come to man for help, so that is what happened to this horse, he ran to the nearest man and stopped; the man got down and caught him.

"We got the cattle settled down and day was breaking when we got into the Alamositas Pasture. Our cook had gone on ahead, had stopped the chuck wagon right close to where we put the herd over the fence. He had breakfast ready, three gallons of black coffee and a quarter of beef cooked and it was pipin' hot. Say, that cook was one of the finest men that ever graced a chuck wagon. His name was Jess Justin.

"Well, when we got through with that breakfast and caught fresh horses, we started on with our herd. We started down one of the Alamositas draws. We had been on the Plains all the time up to now. We were coming off the Plains now into the Canadian Breaks. We followed this draw down until we come to water. There we stopped for noon.

"I and three more of the boys was on herd, that is, we held the cattle until the other boys ate dinner. Sheens and his man turned back for their camp after breakfast, both tired and sleepy, but some wiser. They were two of the finest cowboys that ever jingled a cross L spur.

"By this time we boys on herd got relief and went to dinner. Colonel Boyce was at the wagon when I rode up. He looked me over, and careful. He said, 'Well, Jean, if working and losing sleep one night made me look as onery as it does you, I believe I would go back to the cotton country.' I said, 'Wait a minute, let me get some coffee and one of these beef steaks, and I am rearing to go.' He said, 'If you boys will put this herd into the Rito Blanco Pasture this evening, you can come back to Alamositas ranch house and sleep till eight in the morning.'

"There was plenty of wood and water and a good ranch house at the ranch. We were sure a happy bunch of boys, just then, for a few moments only."

Later Elliston, who worked five months short of ten years for the XIT, helped drive 2500 two-year-olds from the main Texas ranch to the Montana range. The year was 1896 and he was twenty-two years old.

"Not a great deal to say about the trail. In fact, I think it is the easiest part of cow punching. Colonel Boyce counted, that is, he and Albert Boyce, counted out these steers to me.

"The Colonel said, 'Jean, tonight you locate the north star and you drive straight toward it for three months and you will be in the neighborhood of where I want you to turn loose.'

" 'Colonel, some of these cattle is awful weak, and with grass so far, it being the twenty-fifth of April,' I said.

"He said, 'If you can't drive these steers, I will get a man who can. That is what I got you for, to drive these steers and get them fat.'

"There must have been a hundred head we tailed up on the roundup ground. He did not cut out anything only the strays, big jaw, and those with broken legs that had not healed yet. Well, I give him the high ball and told him I was gone. I would see him again late in the fall. That night I located my star all right; so we moved on, eight cowboys, cook, horse wrangler, and boss. That constitutes the outfit. We did not do much driving for the first month, just drifted along until grass rose and cattle got stout. Everything went along all right. Of course we had some storms and some bad nights, but the trail life as a whole is easy compared to ranch life.

"We did not have much trouble until we got to the Yellowstone River. We found it very high and difficult to cross and very dangerous. We were there ten days before we could cross the first herd—and there were five XIT herds on the trail that year. We came very near getting four men drowned at different times. McCanless drove the lead herd. He moved in on the south side of the river on the government reservation at Fort Keogh. The soldiers were there then. The commanding officer gave the XIT Company a permit to cross at this place. However, it is the only crossing in that part of the country that cattle could be crossed from this side of the river, as there chance to be two islands in the river, one being below the other. Being in this position we could swim each current and land the cattle very well.

"We could start into the river on south side quite a ways above the first island, and then swim the cattle over to the first island; then the men would go over in boats. Having crossed our saddle horses with the cattle, we would then catch fresh horses and swim the next channel.

"It was about ten o'clock at night when Milt Whipple and I got our herds across. I never forgot my feelings when we went to cross the last channel—at ten o'clock, just star light, no moon, seven of us men, our saddles and blankets, all wet and heavy, in a small canoe. After we started I slipped my hand over the edge of the boat to see how far it was to the water, it was about four inches. It was an old Swede in charge of the boat. He said, 'Boys, sit steady in the boat or we will all be drowned.' The water was smooth but deep. I wondered when I stepped in that boat if my time had come, but it had not. We landed safely.

"I turned my herd loose eighty miles north of Miles City, Montana, on Cedar Creek; then brought the outfit back to Miles City and waited there until all five of the XIT outfits got there. All of the outfits was turned over to McCanless to bring back to Texas."

Alec Sevier thought he was being relieved of work when in late spring 1904 he was taken off farming for the XIT and sent to Bovina to gather a range herd. But from the very beginning things got off on the wrong foot. The first night on the way down to Bovina it rained. The next morning the plains were so soft that the wagon wheels sank and could not be moved. To lighten the wagons, the beds were packed on the horses, "and of all the bucking, it come off when those old horses were turned loose with the beds."

The next night the crew was at Mustang Windmill. Sevier looked down the draw to see a little sorrel named Sox com-

ing up riderless. In a few minutes Sod Brown, one of the outfit, appeared walking.

"Where did he throw you?" asked Sevier.

"Somewhere between the first and second jump—I can't
tell exactly," retorted Brown.

Later that night their horses stampeded and ran over a
wire fence, cutting themselves rather badly. Some had to be
exchanged with John Armstrong, the Bovina boss.

But the cattle did get picked up. The first night out the
men bedded the steers at the head of Mojares Canyon, and
those who could stretched out for the night.

"We had not more than got to sleep when one of the boys
on guard bulged into camp and yelled, 'All out! The herd
is running.'

"Of course that meant to see who could get there first
among cowboys. Me, Baker, and Walker left together. Huggins was left behind—he missed the herd and never showed
up until just before day. Ed was nearsighted and a little hard
of hearing, which accounted for his mistakes at night. He
was not a shirk by any means.

"We only drive about five miles the next day, and rested
the herd, and they gave us no more trouble. When we got
to the Canadian River it was up about two or three feet, and
those South Plains cattle had never seen a stream of water,
and we sure had some time getting them into it. This was
at George Crossing. There was a bluff below the ford about
eight or ten feet high and then a ledge fifteen or twenty
feet wide out to the water, which was about one foot below
this ledge, which ran back into the main bluff about fifty
yards down the river. About twenty head of cattle went down
on this ledge and would not take the water, which was running into the narrows and deep and swift.

"Earl Woods and myself, both good swimmers, thought
it would be fun to jump those cattle off and see them swim.

So we gave our horses to the other boys to lead across, we stripped, tied our clothes to our saddles, and started down this ledge to have some fun. And we had it at our own expense. The first cow we met jumped us in the water and it was in and out from there on down. I don't know as to the fun the cattle had, but it sure was fun to the other boys. We only pushed one steer off to swim the river, which was not much pay for the swimming we had already done, and we still had to swim the river, as the other boys were having too much fun to bring our horses back; but we swam it like a couple of ducks and no questions asked as to depth or high rolls.

"This trail was uneventful until we got to Carrizo Draw in northeast Middle Water Pasture. We camped on the north side of the draw close to lower Carrizo Windmill and as hard a rain as I ever saw fall, fell that nite. Me, Bob Duke, and Ed Huggins was on midnight guard, which ran from eleven until one. The rain had almost quit and we were standing in front of the herd, which had their backs to the rain and were just taking it fine. But that was too easy— something just had to happen. I never knew what it was, but that herd left there right now, and, as we were in the lead to start with, we did not have much trouble in checking them, but it took us some time to quiet them, as they would flush every now and then."

It might have been this same drive on which Worth Jennings won his spurs. He had been freighting from the Escarbada headquarters to Amarillo and had once stayed alone in a bog camp at Dripping Springs, going thirteen days without seeing another human being. He also claimed to have been on the XIT the day the Dust Bowl was born, with the sun lost in the dust at high noon. But in the spring of 1895 Ira Aten had just promoted him to a regular cowhand, and "Boy, was I tickled!"

"Our first roundups we gathered the steer yearlings (about three thousand), then drove them up the trail to Buffalo Springs. They were delivered to Tobe Pitts, boss of the Buffalo Springs Division. On this trip we had a thunderstorm almost every night, and those fool yearlings got the habit of stampeding every night, and it was not uncommon for the whole crew to be out with the herd. When we arrived at the Canadian River she was up, and the boss said, 'Boys, pack a horse light and we will swim the river and go on.'

"The first night over the river the coyotes stole our bacon; so our chuck was rather scant. When we crossed the Denver Railroad about the Matlock Switch, six miles above the present location of Dalhart, we hustled some old cross ties, killed one of those lean yearlings, cut it in half, propped it up, and roasted him, and when it was barbecued as black as the Ace of Spades, with the pine taste very pronounced, we got around it.

"On the return trip we went by the Bravo Division and picked up five hundred bulls. When we reached the Canadian it was still up, and we had difficulty in getting them to take the water. When they were out in swimming water, every man quit his horse and grabbed a bull by the tail and hung on until we reached shallow water. When we crossed the river we found our wagon and cook, who happened to be one of the best wagon cooks that yelled, 'Here it is!' Good ole Pete had gathered lots of plums and had them fixed up every way for Sunday. We killed a fat calf and really forgot our troubles, drifted back to headquarters, proud and unconcerned."

In another chapter Bob Field tells of a June, 1892, snowstorm that threatened to decimate several herds the XIT was moving from Texas to Montana. This setback was only the beginning of the cowpunchers' woes, for weather, including much water, plagued the herds almost all the way up the trail.

"On the fifth of June we had another storm. We had to wire Mr. Al Boyce to come and buy us some more horses so we could continue to go on with our work. With this same herd we had a stampede on Cheyenne River and close to the ole Spade Ranch in the daytime. In some way we lost about three hundred cattle and the cattle running in the timber. Several was crippled and some few killed themselves. We did not miss these cattle for about two days later. Myself and Chickasaw and one more cowhand went back to hunt these cattle and we gathered them about 150 miles from where we lost them, over in Nebraska where they were in a herd-law country and they had the herd lawed. We were over a week from the time we found them until we got them back to the herd. Our ponies were rode down and we suffered both from eats and something to drink. We were lucky enough one night on our way back to get a pen to put our cattle in I still have a large knuckle right now from roping one of these large steers trying to corral them. I guess there are several who remember these bad storms on this trip north.

"On this same trip Ab Owings got washed off his horse and his horse drowned, and we also thought he was drowned, as we lost sight of him in the swift current. He had a quirt on one hand around his wrist and he said he could not swim as the quirt thrown one arm out of use. He floated about two miles down the river. He said he ran into an island that saved his life. We had went so far as to elect another man to take charge of the outfit and he had come boggin in after we had elected the other man and had eaten dinner. He was bareheaded but still had the quirt in his hand.

"The next the OX's crossed their herd, and Johnnie Luce was drowned, the foreman, and was never found; his horse also drowned. The North Platte made lots of the boys want to quit when they ordered us to swim it on a horse.

"Here is a believe it or not. On this same trip we lost three horses on Sunday Creek and they were kinda noted horses. We thought they were stolen and I put in several days hunting them. Next spring when we rounded up on the Canadian River these three horses showed up all together. One of these horses was a grewier [grulla?]* horse and had the map of Mexico put on him with milkweed; the other horse was a brown, branded L on the shoulder and under-bit out of the left ear. He was supposed to have been stolen from the Burnett outfit and sold to the XIT. The other horse was a sorrel branded rafter dot on the left hip. These horses was rode back or come back by themselves, for there was no fences up there then. This was quite a long trip for horses which were lost.

"I really believe these horses made the trip by themselves."

The next year, 1893, Field was back on the trail to the north. In mid-April he left Channing with about a hundred saddle horses. Milt Whipple was in charge, and Field was straw boss. At Buffalo Springs, where the herd was to be gathered, Whipple told Field to take over temporarily.

"Milt caught the train to see his girl, the Papoose, as he called her. I had the dividing up of the horses amongst the boys; we had some hard-pitching horses. We had a young Englishman, whose name was Harry Mulligan. Me, being young and full of life, I had lots of fun seeing the greeners riding these mean horses. I had all the young horses rode on out by the time we got there. We had a little brown mule which we called Billy the Kid, which was very mean to pitch. We called him a salty jackass.

"I roped this mule and was dragging him out, when Mulli-

* A "grulla" is a mouse-colored, bluish-gray horse.

gan, the young Englishman, said, 'Who is going to ride the jackass?' I told him he could ride him if he wanted to, and he replied that, 'I fancy that I can sit aboard him.' I told him that if he really wanted him he could have him, but that I really aimed to give him to Charley Capel. Charley said for me to give him to Harry if he would take him. Harry said that he wanted him, as it would be fun for him to ride a little jackass like that. So they proceeded to saddle him up, which was a job. Harry Mulligan had a very fine saddle, six-shooter, and an overcoat. The Englishman said after getting his saddle on him that he had his jackass most covered up, that he would be no trouble to ride. When he got on this donkey, he certainly did pitch and threw this Englishman off behind him and kicked him in the stomach as he was coming down.

"When I got to him he looked like a dead man. I sat down and rolled him up in my lap and began to fan him and hollered for the cook to bring some water. The cook was Celso Trujillo. He ran up throwing a whole bucket of water on the Englishman, getting me wet too. He stepped back and said, 'Bobbie, he is sure enough dead and I want his six-shooter and you can have his overcoat,' and he guessed Mr. Whipple would get the saddle. But in a few minutes Harry began to come to. So we loaded him on the wagon and fixed a bed for him to ride on the rest of the day.

"The wagon was just leaving camp ground, Mr. A. G. Boyce and George Findlay drove up and asked me where Whipple was and I told him that he would be over to the roundup. And he asked me if I wasn't some late in getting off with my outfit and I told him the mule Billy the Kid had thrown off a man and kicked him and killed him for a few minutes.

"Mr. Boyce asked me who it was and I told him that it was that dam Englishman who was sent down from Chicago to learn the cow business. Mr. Findlay spoke up and said that I should have not put him on a mule that he had not rode much. I told him that I had rather get a dam Englishman who was sent down from Chicago to learn the cow business killed than a white man. I did not know that Mr. Findlay was an Englishman. [He wasn't; he was a Scotsman.] He surely did get mad when I said that. He told me that I was entirely too smart and did not see why Mr. Whipple would leave an outfit with a young man like me, and I was discharged. He said that 'I am Mr. Findlay of Chicago and have charge of the trail outfits.'

"I told him that he did not hire me and that he could not fire me. It was Whipple who hired me and he was the only man who could fire me.

"Mr. Findlay then went on up to the roundup and told Whipple that he had fired me. Mr. Whipple said, 'He is the only man on the outfit that has been over the trail.' Whipple said, 'I do not know whether you can fire this boy or not, for he is good. He did not mean any harm by putting that Englishman on Billy the Kid; that is customary to put greenhorns on bad horses.' They had quite an argument over me, but Whipple outtalked him and I got to go up the trail in 1893. Mr. Findlay paid us all off on Cedar Creek, Montana, on the first day of August. He still was all swelled up at me. However, I went ahead and worked for them, gathering beef cattle until the snow began to fall. I then quit and went to Chicago to see the World's Fair."

One of the last of the XIT cowboys to handle cattle was Steve Dugger. In the winter of 1911 R. L. Duke sent Dugger to Trujillo Camp to preside over five thousand four-year-olds. It was a hard winter. Cattle would drift, and the quartet of men at the camp would fan out to bring them back to feed them oil cake. Once they were snowed in for three days, with drifts piled so high and frozen so hard that when the men finally emerged, they rode over the tops of the barbed-wire fences. The grass was so thickly covered that the cattle could get nothing to eat. All the cattle went on feed, and the men were busy unloading cake that the company rushed in.

Earlier that year Dugger had gathered a shipping herd to take to Channing. Once he and his companions had gathered their herd, they branded between five and six hundred a day. The outfit was running two cow wagons at the camp.

"C. B. Alford, he took about three thousand calves with his wagon, started near Rito Blanco Ranch with them. The first night he left the other wagon with them, Mr. Moore told me and several other cowboys to go over to C. B. Alford's wagon and stand guard the first night, as these calves were very wild and hard to hold.

"We went over. C. B. Alford said I could sleep in his bed until midnight and stand guard from midnight until daybreak. He would stand guard the first part of the night with the other boys. It come up a bad snowstorm after dark, and the calves stampeded and got away. Mr. Alford came in and woke me, told me to go stand horse guard for one hour—there would be enough boys to stand one hour apiece.

"I got on my night horse; I had him saddled and a stake rope near the wagon. My night horse was about as bad as some of my saddle horses. It was very dark, and so he had to get his head down and do a little rodeo work before he could go to the horses. I did not know where they were, it was snowing and blowing so bad. I told the other cowboy he could go in and I would stand guard, as the calves had stampeded and got away. He asked me where the wagon was at; I told him right back across the hill, but I didn't know where the hill was."

If Dugger or the other cowboy ever found the hill, or the wagon, he left no account. Thirty-six years after an eighteen-year-old Will Rogers made a hand for the Spring Lake Division of the XIT in 1898, he would remember with pleas-

ure his herding days on plains that were "the prettiest country I ever saw in my life, as flat as a beauty-contest winner's
stomach and prairie lakes scattered all over it." He had
helped trail a herd to western Kansas "and there wasn't a
house or chicken in the whole country. . . . And mirages! You
could see anything in the world—just ahead of you."* Or
like Dugger, you could see nothing at all—not even what
you were looking for, not a hill, not a hand, not a herd.

* P. J. O'Brien, *Will Rogers* (Philadelphia, John C. Winston
Company, 1935), p. 121.

"I have no idea how many there was"

ROUNDUP

ROUNDUPS are supposed to have ceased with the
coming of barbed wire fencing—or just when the XIT was
getting started. But some August when you visit Dalhart for
the annual XIT reunion, try telling some of the old hands
that the last real roundup was held in the middle 1880's. Tell
them, but check your exits first, for as recently as the later
days, when the XIT was liquidating its cattle holdings, it was
not unusual for the wagon to go out with the men to begin
gathering and moving when the brush in the brakes would
start greening in April and not to return till the wagon made
tracks through four-inch Christmas snow.

No cow-tending function was more precisely named than

the act of rounding up. Swinging out in a series of wide circles, the cowboys gradually compressed the cattle within
those circles until they had them gathered at one or more central spots. Often the XIT ran at least two roundup locations,
one working east of Tascosa and moving westward, the other
working far to the west, even into New Mexico, and moving
its cattle to the eastward.

Like the other facets of ranch life, rounding up from year
to year was a repetitive experience, but only in the larger
view. The specific cowboy at the specific moment participated
in events or witnessed acts that to him were unique, and his
memory fastened upon and magnified his experiences until
in retrospect each roundup assumed an individuality and ex-
clusiveness never to be met again.

Two things, for instance, stand out in J. W. Standifer's
mind as he writes of his taste of roundups. One is a day in
which he helped brand four hundred calves, an accomplish-
ment which he thinks set a record. His other memory is of a
spring roundup in which the crew fought snow for several
days before they could get down to work.

"Jack Farwell was my wagon boss. There was every type of
man working there at that time owing to Boyce's recent wage
cut from thirty-five to twenty-five dollars for regular cowhands. All the old boys had just quit as I began working. At
this time the whole ranch was stocked with South Texas
Longhorn cattle, with the exception of three or four hundred
head of black Polangus cows that was kept at Buffalo Springs.
These few head of blooded cows was the nest egg from which
the many thousand head of black muley cattle grew in later
years.

"This same year they decided to turn Buffalo Springs into
strictly a steer division, and that was part of our work that
spring and summer to gather steers of all ages from all the
southern divisions and turn them loose at Buffalo Springs. I

have no idea how many there was, but there were several thousand anyway."

It was at another roundup that Standifer witnessed a scene that seared deeply into his memory.

"Lots of the cattle were badly affected with aronia, a skin disease on the order of mange—the hair would come off in big spots. So far they had found no remedy but kerosene. They put them in a shute and sprinkled them with an ordinary flower sprinkler. I remember one day Moore and I had about fifteen or twenty head of the affected animals in a corral, that we had just got through doctoring. There was one that we were going to brand, and in some manner one of them ran through the fire we had built to heat our irons. Of course its kerosene-soaked body caught on fire. It ran back into the bunch a living torch. In less time than it takes to tell it the whole twenty were a mass of flames.

"It was the awfullest sight I ever saw, those poor cows running and bawling, their eyes almost rolling out of their heads in their mortal agony. We opened the gate and let them out, but it did no good. Some of them ran until they fell dead and the others died a much worse way by lingering along for several days."

The hours of night guard duty during roundup were what most impressed Frank Shardelman, who as this is written, is still going strong in Washington state. Teams of two to four men stood two-hour watches, starting at eight o'clock in the evening. Weather, size of herd, kind of cattle (whether cows or beeves), and disposition of herd (whether for beef stock, for range, or for beef cattle for shipment) determined the size of the night guard. It was "my luck," he writes, "as long as I worked for the XIT [to have] third guard [as] my call: 12 to 2 A.M., those nervous hours—change in storms, stillness, and piercing starlight stampedes. You get the works during the season on them hours, good or bad.

"[In 1908] I broke a pair of horses for my swing team. That filled out a beautiful six-horse freight team and was used on the roundup wagon in 1908. R. L. told me that it was one of the best pulling teams he ever saw. I still have their picture taken hitched up to the roundup wagon.

Their names: Lead team: Curly and Sawyer
Swing team: Morgan and Dewey
Wheel team: Washington and Lexington.

"The spring of 1908 the roundup started in April and we began working at Cheyenne Lake near Tascosa, working north and holding beef stock to ship north for summer range in Montana. Florence Moore had not been with the wagon the latter part of 1907 on account of an injured back, and Egbert Ramsay had finished the season as wagon boss. Now Moore was back, also part of the old hands and some new men.

"At Four Mile we were given our full string of horses; each man had from twelve to fifteen horses, according to what he done. Classified they were—circle horses, cutting horses, roping horses, and night horses. Most were circle horses, as they were used for making the drives, and consisted of anything from a raw bronco to any horse that could take you for a long ride. The others were trained for their duty. To give an idea how horses were named, I will list the names of the horses I had while with the XIT:

Slippers	Ream
London Bill	Battleaxe
F. M. Boy	Dynamite
Heavy Tail	Sitting Bull
Si Bean	Charley at the Wheel
M Bar	Lee Morris
Dart	Black Cat and Vinegar Roan

"Multiply that by thirty or more men for a roundup wagon outfit. It took lots of horses and some strange names. So the work went on seven days a week, always on the move—and don't omit the cook, who moved his camp site nearly every day and prepared meals for that hungry bunch on a potrack with Dutch ovens. Hats off to such men as Jim McLemore, Hugh Hampton, Sam McBride, and many others that cooked for the XIT.

"I left the XIT the summer of 1908 at Perico, when we moved in with a large herd to ship north.

"A few days before reaching Perico, Dynamite took one of his bucking spells, for which he was famous. After a few tries he threw me, saddle and all, in a pile on my head. It hurt my neck but I resaddled and went on. That night my night horse, F. M. Boy, stuck both front feet in a hole while running, fell and broke his neck, and almost broke mine.

"I stayed with the wagon until we got to Perico, bandaging my neck with my muffler, but it pained me so I quit and went to a doctor, who found a vertebra out of place, and advised me to quit riding. I let him twist my neck and doctor me for a while, when he said the vertebra was back in place but not to ride for a while.

"I bid the XIT goodby and went to New Mexico, then a territory and finished the year at Cimarron. I knew you did not want any loose bones when such horses as Dynamite, Sitting Bull, Charley at the Wheel, and Lee Morris started cradling with you."

To J. A. Smiley in later years the XIT was just about the best outfit for which any man could ever hope to work. He respected his division boss, Henry Eubanks, as a "real cow-man and the best trail man I ever saw. He could water more cattle in a small lake of water and never get it muddy than any man I ever saw." From the time he first saw the Yellow Houses in the spring of 1888, Smiley thought its pasture "was a beautiful sight to look at, most all kinds and colors of wild flowers." In May of that spring his group started to

work the Yellow Houses, or No. 7 Division, as they sometimes called it.

"The No. 6 boys and their foreman, Frank Yearwood,
came down from Spring Lake to help us round up and brand.
I have worked cow outfits, but the Yellow Houses Ranch was
the best-fixed ranch I ever worked for. It once was headquarters was the reason it was fixed better than the other
divisions.

"We had a small beef pasture to hold the steers in as we
cut them out of the roundup each day. It was a little ways
northwest of the ranch. At nearly every roundup ground
there was a small horse pasture and a camp for a line rider or
a windmill oiler.

"So 'Uncle Henry,' as we called him, says to us boys, 'Put
the horses and steers in the horse pasture,' and we would go
to bed after we got through spinning yarns. We used cow
chips to cook and brand with. If the people who read this
don't know what cow chips is we will just leave them
guessing.

"I don't just remember how many days we were rounding
up the Yellow Houses Pasture. After we got through Uncle
Henry and the boys went up to Spring Lake with Frank Yearwood to work the Spring Lake Pasture. Uncle Henry sent me
to help a stray man with his cattle, and had to go east through
Horseshoe Pasture, owned by the Snyders, and put the cattle
on what was called 'outside,'* where Lubbock, Plainview,
Floydada, Lockney stand now. That part was full of antelope
and mustangs.

"Then after we got the cattle on the outside we went back
to the south, Snyders camp, and got supper and stayed all
night. They had a dugout there. We made a bed down on the
outside, as we were accustomed to do sometimes. In the

* Outside the XIT boundaries, that is.

night a Norther blowed up, we had our heads to the north and it blowed the cover all off of us. We got up and spent the night in the dugout. Next morning we was up early. Then I had to go to Spring Lake that day facing the norther. I had done throwed my coat away, didn't think I'd ever need it again any more. It must have been somewhere from the twentieth to the twenty-fifth of May. I rode all day—it must have been fifty miles or more—and the horse I was on was locoed.

"Maybe I had better explain this loco business. Loco is a weed that comes up early in the spring before the grass comes up. Stock will eat it and the more they eat the more they want. They will hunt it just like a dope fiend man will hunt morphine. If they don't get too bad they sometimes get over it and get fat but they never get active any more.

"Well, I rode into the Spring Lake Ranch about sundown, tired and hungry. The cook had a good warm supper—plenty of black coffee and sour-dough biscuits. Well, we set around and talked cows and horses, as each one of us had a horse that could outrun the other fellow's horse.

"Next morning we started to working Spring Lake Pasture. Our first roundup was at the Ranch. We branded in the corral. Uncle Henry appointed me to rope calves that day and Frank Yearwood appointed a man from his bunch of waddies. Well, we run neck and neck with very few miss. That was when the Blocker loop was first interdused on the Plains. I had practised it a lot and Uncle Henry knew it. So finally there come a calf on the wrong side of me, nearly the full length of my rope from me. I taken a long chance, twisted the twine on him. He went high in the air. It was a pure dee accident, that was, but there wasn't anybody knew it but me. So I didn't let on but it was science; so they lost sight of the Spring Lake man. And he had me skinned a city block on a wide open rope, but he just couldn't twist the Blocker loop.

"We made one roundup at the Alamositas Line Camp. There was a waddie riding line there, and he was just living like folks. He had put him up a cow, and had him a churn, had butter and buttermilk. He was just living royal, but when he come home that night his milk and butter had all disappeared. Of course I didn't have anything to do with that.

"We didn't have as good a time working the Spring Lake Pastures like the Yellow Houses did; so we had to stand guard. When we rounded up near the Sod House it rained one day, and we didn't do much but ride broncs. The Spring Lake outfit had a nigger cook called Bob. They managed to get old Bob on a bronc. It kept us guessing who would win, old Bob or the bronc. Finally the bronc lost. Old Bob had just about give it up when the bronc gives out. We didn't have a nigger in our outfit and old Bob was the only one on the XIT, as far as I know. He was a good cook or he wouldn't have been on No. 6. We finished up the Spring Lake Pasture; then we went back to the Yellow Houses to clean up the bunch of steers so we could drive them to the general beef pasture.

"We come back to Alamositas, and as my feet was beginning to itch for adventure and I was taking the New Mexico fever, I drawed my little roll. While we were there at headquarters I saw young Al Boyce. He was a kid then about ten years old, a-riding a pony around in the yard. He was killed by the same man that killed his father. This was after he had grown up to be a man."

Bob Beverly tells how in the spring of 1894 he helped gather two-year-old steers to turn over to the several trail bosses to drive to Montana. In all he turned over four herds of about 2500 cattle each, including one to Scanless John McCanless, a boss who lingers in everyone's memory but who left no recollection himself.

Beverly recalls that as the herds moved out over the hills north of Buffalo Springs, "there were very few fences from there to the Yellowstone River." And ringing in each trail boss's ears was a stern admonition from A. G. Boyce "to never let a steer look back until they had crossed the Yellowstone."

Happy to participate in roundup by being allowed to treat scabby cattle was Alec Sevier, who had spent his first several months on the XIT working over every windmill at Rito Blanco. When he finished that chore he was sent to bog camp about April Fool's Day. It had not rained since September and would not rain for another three months. The last of June found Sevier still pulling bog, skinning cattle, and eating dust. No wonder then that in the fall of 1904 he was excited about being assigned to dip every head of cattle on the Rito Blanco Division.

"We would dip one pasture at a time, take them back, and round up another and dip them. We run the Rito Blanco Pasture cattle through last at McGee dipping vat (One inspector said that the XIT run seven thousand head through McGee before breakfast, it was so big), stayed there that night, and turned the horses in Baldface Pasture. It was small and we would not have to stand guard. Manley Walker, Bob Baker, and myself were on rustle next morning. We got in a little after sunup with the horses and found out Bob Duke had laid off four men, including the cook, Matt Williams, a little short Negro. Bob Baker said it was a good thing we were on rustle or we might have got fired.

" 'Yes,' old Matt said, 'Mister Bob slept cold last night, but got up wahm, dis mahnin'.' "

But Bob Duke's "wahm" feeling persisted, and Sevier was soon sent packing. He tells of his departure and his survival:

"We moved from McGee well to the Kimball corrals, took down some old fence, and fenced some haystacks, went in to Rito Blanco, and turned the horses loose. The next morning Bob came to the bunkhouse and told us he would have to lay

off some more men. He says, 'I'll give you some checks with a
hog on it so you can get back in the spring.' We told him if
the hog didn't pace we wouldn't ride him. So we rolled our
beds and went to Channing that day on a freight wagon
driven by Shorty Simpson, the cook that took old Negro
Matt's place.

"I didn't lose much time. I took the line rider's place at
Channing while he was on vacation, and then took the windmills in Charley Johnson's place while he took Christmas.
Charley asked me to take the mills when the line rider came
back, and if he got back on time and I took the windmill
wagon he wanted to extend his vacation a week or so, as he
had a peach down at Bellvue, and told me to wire him in case
everything was O.K. The line rider got back on time and I
took the windmill wagon and sent Charley this simple wire:
'Charley, stay with the peach. I've got the mills. Alec.' When
Charley came back about the fifteenth of January he told me
that the fool wire caused more questions to be asked than
anything he ever heard of.

"I then went to the farm. Lee Landers was farm boss. Me
and Bill Caldwell fed the thoroughbred Herefords until the
first of March. I hauled cake, salt, cottonseed, and corn from
Channing to Rito Blanco and the Bull Camp and fell out of
the wagon twice.

"Once right in a two-mile gate. I had got out and opened
the gate, got back in the wagon to drive through, and was
stooped over unwrapping the lead lines off the standard. The
leader swung to the right and hung break beam on the gate
post and brought the wagon to a sudden stop, but I didn't
stop—I went out over the right front wheel. Sam, a blue stal-
lion, the near wheel horse, Sampson, a big black on off
wheel, Rubberneck, a tall bay on the near lead, and Drome-
dary, a tall blue-gray in the off lead—I believe they were the
finest team I ever pulled a line over. They were fat and sleek

all the time and as true as steel, and stout. They were like the Arkansawyer's bulls that could pull hell and break iron.

"But the XIT was noted for good horses and pretty ones, and also for ugly cowpunchers, of which I am a fair sample with plenty of company."

Ugly, Sevier may have been, but to be bromidic, if "pretty is" as the saying says it is, then no cowpuncher and no cow-pony were ugly, for silhouetted against a spacious palette they worked in harmony and rhythm, a blend of art and music, giving to each roundup now the rapid but steady spacing of an equine *toccata*, now the alternation of purpose of a *rondo,* and finally the crashing inevitability of the *coda.* A well-conducted roundup had all the logic and all the mathematical progression of a well–thought-out composition—and to those who experienced it, all the satisfaction and sense of completeness too.

STAMPEDES

NO ONE EVER SAW a herd of cattle get up and take off on a stampede. One minute they are bedded down quietly; a moment later they are *all* running.

J. W. Armstrong, on night duty, learned this. Every time he made his round of the herd he had to swing out to circle an old steer bedded down out of line. About the tenth time Armstrong swung out, he spat in the old fellow's direction.

The next instant he was chasing an entire herd.

On another night Jim Sparks lit a cigaret. Four thousand cattle went wild. Out of their "hot rolls" came the hands, wide-awake at once, as the train of steers roared by, looking fifty feet high. Three of the men, "britches in their hands," jumped to the top of the wagon, waving their pants in the air and yelling, "Hi! Hi!"

"I can see them now, and still chuckle at the ridiculous sight they made during such a serious moment," recalls Blue Stevens.

Again, J. W. Standifer and Rainy Way had the watch at Rito Blanco. The steers were fat, awaiting shipment, and were corralled. It was a quiet, routine night, though clouds were gathering and the wind was freshening. Suddenly came a clap of thunder.

Down went the fence, and out streamed the cattle.

"As none of the other boys had a horse up, it felt to us two to do what we could," Standifer remembers.

"I got the general direction in which they were headed, and thought I would try to get in front of them and check them. After I had ridden about two miles I heard them coming down a draw in front of me. They were travelling in a fast trot about seven or eight abreast. I had no idea how many had already passed. But I remembered that this draw ran into a pretty-good-sized creek about a half mile farther on. I also knew that they would have to slow up to cross; so I hurriedly rode ahead and crossed the creek, and came up to where they were crossing.

"I cut off what had already gone by, and without very much trouble I held the rest on the opposite bank until they had all crossed. It was some time before the tail end caught up. I held them on a nearby flat until morning. I had no idea how many I had, but when daylight came I saw that I must not have cut off very many. When the boys came we counted them and were only about two hundred short, and we found them about four miles farther on, where they had gone into another herd of cattle headed for New Mexico, that were being held over night. So we didn't lose a cow, just a little energy cutting them out of that trail herd and taking them home."

Stampedes look good on a movie screen. To a cowhand, however, they ranked with fire as just about the most unwelcome event that could take place, enjoyable only to talk about later, the way an appendectomy eventually becomes eligible reminiscence. Cowboys tending herd invariably ran short of sleep and treasured every moment spent horizontal. Stampedes knocked the daylights out of the sleeping routine, and once begun, were a chore that had to be seen through to solution, regardless of exposure, fatigue, or hunger.

More than that, stampedes were dangerous. Riding like a devil through the night, intent more on heading a herd than in watching for shadowy hazards, the cowboy was narrowing the odds in favor of his attaining a serene old age. A horse's hoof, a prairie-dog mound, the right angle of contact—and one stumbling horse might pitch the best rider into oblivion. Living with peril though he did, the cowboy nevertheless saw little reason to ask for a shorter life, and riding pell-mell after a stampeding herd was asking for just that.

Besides, stampedes were expensive. There was always the possibility of cattle crushed or drowned or torn apart by blind runs over the edges of sheer bluffs. Scattered cattle might require hours, or even days, of search for recovery. If they went in the wrong direction, you had to reckon in the time necessary to bring them back to where all the trouble started. And, of course, mad midnight dashing over the countryside added no meat to the creatures' bones.

When Mack Huffman came to the XIT in July of 1885, he intended to remain only six months. Thirteen years later he was still there.

"Went to work," he says. "Never seen home for a few years. Worked continuously."

During one of those continuous years, he was taking thirty-one hundred steers north along the Frio. Steve Karr was his wagon cook. It was ten o'clock, and life on the range was tranquil. The next thing he remembers, the cattle were coming toward the mess wagon, and Steve Karr was standing on the footboard alongside the wagon bed, holding to the bows with each hand, hollering, "Boys, God damn it! Cattle stampeding!"

Huffman ignored Steve, and headed instead for the lead steers. But before he could get going he spotted Jack Bradford trying to board his horse.

As Bradford went up in the stirrup, the cattle beat by him and knocked him to the ground into a cactus cluster. Huffman had no time to see to Bradford, but went after his cattle. First things first. When later he returned, he had no difficulty finding Bradford, because the man lay groaning. The cattle hadn't hurt him, but the prickly pear had. While the other boys held Bradford down, Huffman probed his wounds by lantern light.

The next day was spent tallying and the next night resting. That is, until four o'clock in the morning, when Steve Karr started his morning cook fire. Off went the cattle again, and up on the table of the mess wagon went Steve, "holding to upper stories of box, hollering and stomping, 'Boys, cattle's stampeding.'" Away went Huffman.

"I reached the lead of the herd just as they came to the old Tascosa-Springer trail. We jumped it like it was a plowed furrow. Stopped the herd O.K. Next morning was loading our herd, ran over where we crossed the old trail. A fine steer lay dead—and made it across, fell, and as the roaring herd passed over him broke his neck."

Another story with Huffman in the center is told by Bob Beverly. As Beverly was proceeding with a large herd Huffman, with a smaller bunch, caught up along the Canadian

River. They spent the night, Beverly's group on the north side and Huffman's on the south. The next morning Huffman prepared to swim his group over.

"Huffman rode up on the banks of the Canadian River, pulled his hat off, and hollered, 'Three cheers for six bold and dashing cowboys and fifty-seven hundred XIT steer yearlings,' grabbed his horse with his spurs, and jumped him off a bank into the Canadian River, and went out of sight under the muddy water. But his horse came to the top about a hundred feet from the bank and struck out for the south side, where his men had all gone ahead of him. Such was the men that . . . in a recent article was called 'Montgomery Ward cowboys.'

"Then it was up to the six bold and dashing cowboys to deliver the steers to the Agua Frio Pasture, east of Buffalo Springs; that being for summer range for the steer yearlings and wintering them in the more broken country along the line south to Carrizo Camp and Farwell Park Pasture.

"The second night, as the moon was shining bright, Dick Estes got off his horse and his horse gave himself a shake, rattling his saddle, and it looked like the whole north Plains country was covered with running steer yearlings. I being on the opposite side from Dick, of course the most of them came my way. The next morning I was singing to a bunch of about four thousand just about where Rehm is now and about nine o'clock Webb and the other boys came to me with the rest of the herd, of fifty-seven hundred. I asked Dick where he went to after the yearlings run. He said, 'I went to sleep. Where do you think I went!' "

One final stampeding recollection, this by Arch Sneed, then only seventeen years old, gives an idea of the uncertain quality of the reckless chase through a violent night. Sneed had come into Dalhart in late June 1898 with twenty-seven hundred two-year-olds to be shipped to the Montana range. The steers had a reputation for restiveness, for on their way in from Bovina they had indulged themselves in several small stampedes. But now they were safely bedded down a mile and a half north of the railroad roundhouse, and Colonel A. C. Boyce himself was nearby to see that Sneed and his companions had them in the pens by sunup.

Sneed was to stand second guard, going on about midnight.

"When I was called to go on guard the man who was to go with me was Claude McCracken, now of Clarendon, Texas, and there was coming up a cloud and storm; it was thundering. We loped up to the herd in our usual manner and said, 'We got 'em,' which was the customary remark when we relieved a guard. But Jim Hill, from the Indian Territory, an old cowboy and an old-timer who had had much experience, remarked, 'I don't like the looks of that cloud; so we will stay with you a while.' So the four of us scattered out around the herd, most of them laying down and quiet at the time.

"It was only a very short time, as I remember it, until the storm broke, and there came a loud clap of thunder and flash of lightning, and these steers were all up in an instant, just flash off like a bunch of quail. They run north toward Buffalo Springs, and me being on the south side of the herd at the time they run threw me behind the run. It commenced pouring down rain instantly almost, and lightning fast. I could see those men when the lightning would flash, and the cattle were running like an ocean. I could see the yellow slickers of the men when the lightning flashed as they ran on their horses putting on their slickers and trying to get to the lead of the herd. Me being behind the herd I was following them as much by the noise as anything else. The cat-

tle running through the blue-stem grass would make a pop-
ping noise and occasionally when a flash of lightning came
I could see yellow slickers of these men.

"We were going north toward Buffalo Springs, as I said,
and there wasn't a fence for fifteen or twenty miles in that
direction. Now, I had no idea of the distance we traveled and
was blinded by the flashes of lightning and the darkness and
was confused on direction, but suddenly there came a long
glaring flash of lightning—stood light for several seconds—
and instead of being behind the herd I was up beside the
lead cattle running and I was almost with the lead cattle. So
I lammed the spurs into my horse to go up to the front and
circle them back, which was customary in a running herd of
cattle, to throw them into a mill.

"Just when I spurred my horse to go to the lead cattle, I
was about to the lead cattle when I struck a five-wire fence
which was the outside fence somewhere about where Kofer's
dairy is now. My horse and I went plumb over the fence
outside; we fell clear over the fence. The rain was falling
hard by that time and when I tried to get up I couldn't; my
right leg seemed numb. I didn't feel any pain, so I didn't
think I was hurt. I don't think any cattle struck the fence;
my going over the fence turned the cattle and they milled
and bawled there and when it lightened I could see them.
I was laying on the other side of the fence and the cattle were
milling in a circle and bawling. The noise of my striking the
fence had turned them back and throwed them into a mill.

"Had there been anybody with me at that time we could
have probably held them. As it was, we lost the entire herd.
What happened was these boys that had left in the lead had
been turning them back all the time to the right and had
made a complete circle almost and come back to the outside
fence about three miles from where we started. They had

run their horses down and had lost the herd at the time they
turned them back to me.

"I tried to get up, as I said before, and my leg was numb
and I couldn't walk on it. It lightened and I saw a cow trail
with water in it and I suddenly got very thirsty. That was the
first I realized or thought I was bleeding, as I was not feeling any pain at all. I dragged myself over to the cow trail
and got a drink of water. In crawling over I felt my leg at
the knee with a kind of stinging feeling and numb. I had on
two pairs of heavy California pants; had slept in one pair
and pulled the other pair on over them when called to go on
guard. I had also pulled on a slicker and a pair of heavy H. J.
Justin boots, which came to my knees. I found that my pants
were cut and torn completely off above the knee and top of
my boot was cut off about half way from the knee to the
ankle. Above the knee was a gash cut to the bone about seven
or eight inches long clear across and the wire had sawed
into the bone. That was the only place I was hurt, was on
the leg. The heavy pants and boot top had saved me.

"I could see the lights of Dalhart all the time, and I think
now I must have passed out for a while, because it didn't
seem long until daylight. I got very sick and at daylight I
could see the chuck wagon over there and only one horse in
sight. This horse was ridden by the horse wrangler, who was
Bud Farmer, now of Young County, Texas. He saw my horse
standing over there and came to me. My horse wasn't seriously hurt, just cut all over but not seriously. Farmer came to me
and mashed the fence down and fastened it with his horn
strings and saddle rope so he could get his horse over and
got me on my horse and led my horse hobbling, and we went
back to the wagon, where some of the boys came in to the
wagon. They had lost their horses too.

"[Farmer] put my saddle on another horse and led him

into town to Lee Cannon's saloon . . . and called the cabman, which was Henry Tandy . . . and he hauled me to Dr. Hedrick. He wasn't out of bed, but got up and went with us to Mrs. Lyons' and got Fred Lyon, who was his office boy, just about twelve or fourteen years old and weighed about two hundred pounds, and we went to the doctor's office, which was back of McGee's Drug Store.

"The doctor strapped me to an operating table and had Fred Lyon sit on my head while he sewed up my leg. He wouldn't give me any anaesthetic of any kind, no local or otherwise. In fact, he said that I had laid out in the grass and weeds and rain so long there might be poison infection. He sewed up my leg with a needle like I had seen to sew up sacks at a thresher. He put a block on one side of the gash and shoved the needle through to the other side and tied the knot. He took eight or nine stitches in this manner. All I could do was holler as he had me strapped down and a two-hundred-pound boy on my head. Fred was his regular office boy and wore a sailor collar, knee pants, and button shoes.

"They took me to a room at Mrs. Pittman's, which was over a two-story building. . . . I stayed there a week before I could hobble around much. Colonel Boyce came to see me two or three times during the time I was there; everybody was nice to me. My leg healed very fast. The first day I was up hobbling around I met Colonel Boyce on the street and he asked me how I was getting along and I said fine. He told me there was a train of empty stock cars ready to leave for Middle Water, where the XIT's were loading cattle and for me to go out with those empties and to report to Joe Armstrong, foreman of Bovina, who was then in charge of shipping at Middle Water, and to accompany his shipment to Glendive, Montana, while I was unable to ride. They were shipping the steers to their northern range. I was on pay, as the Company let my pay go on, as I was injured, and he paid my expenses and sent me with this train of cattle."

A rampaging heard of white-eyed stampeding steers must have been a spectacular and memorable scene, epic in its wildness. It provided fierce adventure, never to be forgotten and to be improved with each re-telling, adventure full of awful dark nights, their blackness and silence split open by lightning and hail, mad cattle bellowing and pounding, cowboys yelling and riding off in all directions, and wall-eyed night horses doing their best to get up front and start the cattle to milling. It must indeed have been thrilling.

But undoubtedly it was best in retrospect.

RUSTLING

RUSTLING, whether it be outright thievery, care-less eating of a neighbor's beef, or mavericking, was never considered very charitably by the XIT. There had been a time in the West when small-time cattle stealing had been viewed with a certain tolerance, and undoubtedly a number of later respectable spreads received their starts from calves that somehow got lost from their mothers.

But with the coming of fencing and the introduction of Northern and Eastern businessmen, not to mention Scottish syndicates, cattle were looked upon as dollars-and-cents in-ventories and assets and any attempts to reduce that inven-tory without proper replacement was bad bookkeeping pro-

cedure, to say the least. The XIT owners of the 1880's and
thereafter were hardheaded Midwesterners who went into
ranching to collect from an impecunious State of Texas; they
wanted their investment back. Besides, they had obligations
to the other members of their syndicate, both domestic and
foreign. With all the inconveniences of absentee ownership,
they nonetheless insisted on strict accounting; and their in-
sistence spread through the ranch foremen down to the low-
est and loneliest of employes.

In one way the XIT was fortunate. Most of its land was
plains, unbroken and wide-sweeping, with little shelter for
stolen herds or from whining bullets. But there were breaks,
as along the Canadian, with enough hills and ravines and
scrubby growth to encourage the greedy or envious. To the
west was New Mexico Territory, for miles unbroken by
barbed wire, so that a thief could move without hindrance.
And the XIT was huge, a rich and natural target. Stealing
from it was not the crime, not even to a jury of peers, that it
might be from a lesser outfit—although not for a moment
would an XIT hand agree with that assertion. Guarding all
of the XIT all of the time was an impossibility; with such ex-
panse it would still be impossible today.

To a certain extent the ranch was guarded by fear. Along
the western line especially, any unidentified person found
riding in XIT pastures might be shot in advance of questions,
as his mere presence would make him as suspect as a stranger
found nowadays in a private house when a family returned
home. If an outsider had a stray in an XIT pasture, good insurance dictated that he go to the division headquarters and
get an XIT hand to go looking with him.

The XIT never did stamp out rustling, but it did protect
its contents so vigilantly as to discourage all but the most determined. Since it could not always depend on the law, it
sometimes became the law for one or more counties. That it

was highhanded is undeniable; that such highhandedness
taught respect for law in an area where legal enforcement was
frequently inadequate is equally undeniable.

Originally the most common form of stealing was mavericking—the stealing of large unbranded calves, common
enough to be accepted in some areas as custom. At one time
the commissioners court at Tascosa was in the mavericking
business up to its neck, supplying a local restaurant owner
named Scotty Wilson with all the steaks he could sell. The
game ended when the commissioners called on Scotty for
payment. Said Wilson:

"First you stole them; now I steal them. So what?" The
court could not think of an adequate answer.

In the first days the XIT had more trouble from thieves on
the inside of its organization than on the outside. The early
general manager was Colonel B. H. Campbell—"Barbecue"
Campbell, as he was more widely known. Big-faced, over-
bearing, loud-mouthed, personally penurious, and institu-
tionally extravagant, according to J. Evetts Haley, he stocked
the ranch with hands who, to be charitable, were often ques-
tionable. A. L. Matlock, a Montague County lawyer, was sent
to look into Campbell's operations, along with a young Scotsman, George Findlay, from the Chicago office. Mrs. Duke
received from Findlay himself the story of what they
found:*

"Mr. Matlock had saved Campbell's range boss from a
hanging at Vernon, Texas," relates Mrs. Duke. "Mr. Matlock told Mr. Findlay that the boss's being there was evidence
that something was very wrong. Matlock talked with the cowboys, saw men working there, or were on the payroll, who
had been run out of other sections of the country; saw the

* Part of this account is given in detail in Haley, *The XIT Ranch
of Texas*, pp. 100–103.

ranch harboring horse thieves, evidence of theft, and general
lawlessness. Gambling was going on everywhere. They
stopped the cow outfits to gamble on a blanket any place. Mr.
Matlock reported all of this to Chicago. They wanted Mr.
Matlock to run the ranch. He would not take it, but went to
Colorado City and tried to get a man there to run the ranch,
but this man said that he was of more value to his wife and
children than to go to the XIT Ranch and be shot full of
holes.

"Mr. Matlock chose Colonel A. G. Boyce, who was then
delivering cattle from the Snyder brothers and was trying to
water them. They put Colonel A. G. Boyce in charge and
fired almost every man on the ranch, but not all of them. They
had some honest men, among them Frank Yearwood, Mack
Huffman, and some others.

"They began organizing the ranch. The old range boss
with ten gun men rode up to bring an end to the administration of the lawyer. They met, but the ten gun men and their
boss soon left, and it was said that the population of New
Mexico was increased. Barbecue Campbell did not stay long
enough to receive all the cattle. He had fired a tough cowboy,
then took him back. He hooked up a fine team to a buckboard
and 'lit out.' "

"There was still a hard-looking case there," continues
Mrs. Duke. "Mr. Findlay described him to [me] as follows:

" 'I told Boyce he should wear a gun and be ready to use
it,' said Mr. Findlay.

" 'Oh,' said Boyce, 'they are bad but they wouldn't shoot
an unarmed man.'

"Mr. Findlay was standing in the doorway, his hand on his
gun, when the tough character was taking his horse loose
from the hitching post. Colonel Boyce was halfway between
the house and the barn, going to the barn. The tough custo-
mer lifted his gun, starting to point it at Boyce's back. Mr.

Findlay had been watching and he yelled at that moment. The man turned; he was looking into Mr. Findlay's gun.

" 'Drop that gun!' yelled Mr. Findlay. Mr. Findlay got the gun and told him to get out of there.

" 'From what happened down there I know that every ranch manager is in danger all the time,' said Mr. Findlay."

At times the XIT hired sheriffs or Texas Rangers as hands in order that mavericks or brand-burners might be more efficiently handled. Always the XIT co-operated with any law enforcement agency that showed a proper punitive spirit.

One of the longer and more dramatic accounts of such co-operation is related by W. J. Cook, who was stationed at a line camp ostensibly to ride fence. "But that was merely a front," he remembers.

"Our real reason was to keep a lookout for rustlers. Smoke was beginning to boil there and I knew there would be trouble sooner or later.

"In December the fireworks began to pop. The Rangers had two men in jail at Quanah on the charge of rustling. One of the men was 'Arizona Johnny,' but I don't remember his pardner's name. It would mean that justice could be given if someone had nerve enough to go after the evidence, but if we didn't get it the whole thing was shot up. Frank Yearwood explained it all to us as we stood about the fire in the cabin. We were all men, and some of us with families to think of. It wasn't a glorious thing at all but it had to be done. We were somber-eyed and quiet, but determined to do our best if we were chosen.

" 'Men,' Yearwood said, 'I'm not going to demand that any of you go. It's a hard trip to make under ordinary conditions, but in this kind of weather and up against what you will have to fight—well, it'll just mean death. There's a frail chance that you can get through, but with the country alive with rustlers and their friends I doubt it.'

The XIT general headquarters in Channing. It looks almost exactly the same fifty years later, except that the saddled white horse has moved on.

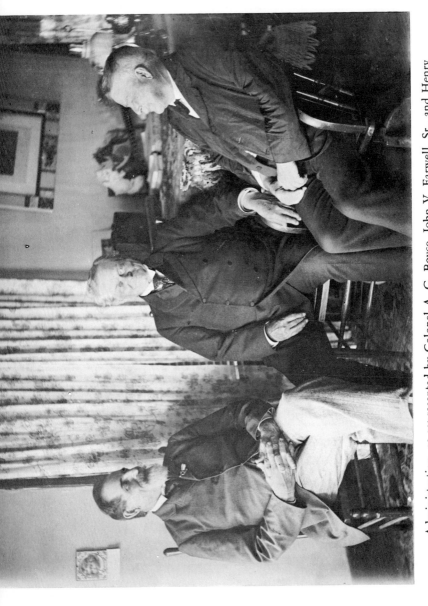

Administration, as represented by Colonel A. G. Boyce, John V. Farwell, Sr., and Henry Stephens. Comments Mrs. Duke: "How funny Mr. Farwell looked when he got bogged."

Chuck time at Yellow Houses. The cart at the right contains "prairie coal," or chips for cooking, in a land that has no wood.

An XIT chuck wagon and potrack.

XIT wagons on the move in Montana. An E. J. Cameron photo.

XIT wagon in camp, Montana, 1906. On the ground, left to right, are Mose Howard, Ed Thompson, T. D. McMakin, Harry Smith (a horse wrangler), Ed Payne (a CK man), M. L. Phipps, and Ed Weisner. Jay Case, the cook, and Bill Quigley (from the Diamond G) are standing. An E. J. Cameron photo.

An XIT version of a caravan. John V. Farwell's party crossing the Canadian in the 1890's.

There is no easy, pleasant way to get a bogged steer out of the Canadian River sand.

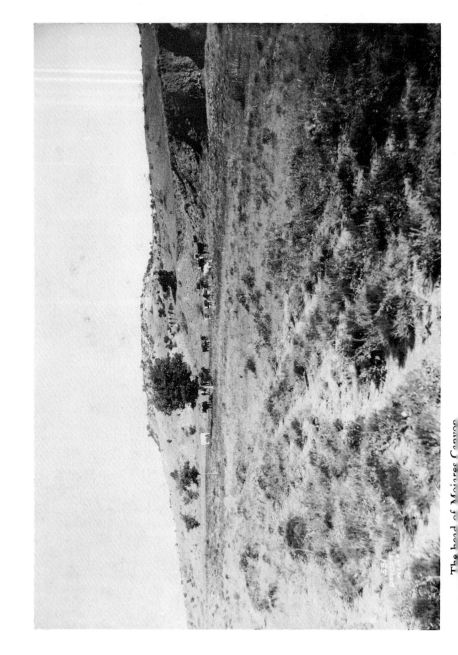

The head of Mojaves Canyon

The Montana hands at Cedar Creek, 1910. An E. J. Cameron photo.

The time to read mail is when you get it, even in a Buffalo Springs hay *vega*. Reading over another's shoulder isn't bad manners but requires good eyes.

Bob Duke in 1895, when he was a simple cowhand unworried by foreman or managerial duties. Note the XIT brand on the horse's flank.

Romero's general store was hardly impressive a half-century ago.

Today it is even less so.

Jim Perry, best cook, best fiddler . . . ?

No XIT horse, in Texas or Montana, ever threw Charlie Clements, left, though two in Colorado did. With him on the Montana range in 1902 are the three Buckley girls—Myrtle, May, and Mable, all girls who could hold a herd and rope a cow—and John K. Marsh, a real top hand.

Waiting outside the bunkhouse. The hats are broad-brimmed and high-crowned, a far cry from the sleek stylized John B.'s of today, but no cowboy would be seen outside without one any more than a lady would have gone to town without gloves.

Feeding the chickens, hardly the thing for a spirited cowboy.

Branding on the Bravo Division, 1900. The fuzziness across the left center is caused by dust, not bad photography. Note the taut line being held on the calf at the extreme left by the horse, and the men on the ground heating the next iron.

A July 4 celebration near Terry, Montana. An E. J. Cameron photo.

Forty years later, old-timers gather in Dalhart to "cool their coffee" with a f
prime stories. From left to right they are (standing) Arch Sneed, Mrs. Dul
Goldie Thomas, Frank Farwell, Charlie Alford, and George Hayden; and (s
ting) Bob Beverly, Mike Crow, Hall Medford, Bill Culbertson, and Bill Aske
Bill Rhew Picture Service.

The Spring Lake Division outfit.

Climbing aboard the hurricane deck of a pony.

Reflections in the water. The spring hole at Alamositas camp.

The remuda in Alamositas, 1898.

Windmill and tank on the Rito Blanco. Space is not a problem.

"We made one roundup at the Alamositas   " (1900)

Like cowboys, cattle get thirsty. Here they wet dry throats at the Kimball Corral of the Rito Blanco Division. The garden in the foreground promises scant yield.

A small herd of Aberdeen Angus cluster around the windmill. Pictures like this explain why in a land mostly as flat as an ironing board, cowboys can break their necks in ten-foot falls while chasing stampeding cattle through a starless night.

6,000 miles . . . plus 800 feet more of white picket fence around the Buffalo Springs headquarters in 1898. Under the bonnet is Mrs. Tobe Pitts, the cows are Black Angus and muley, and the trees are real.

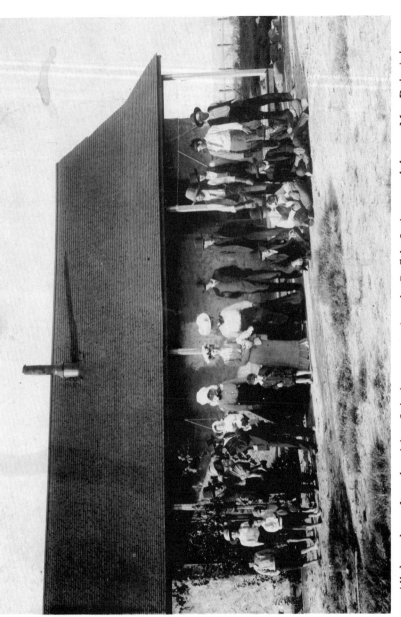

All dressed up after a baptizing. It is August, 1906, at the Buffalo Springs ranch house. Mrs. Duke is be-tween two other women, the one wearing the hat that allows the sun to come in

What to wear to a July 4 to-do at the hotel in Channing.

Sometimes cowboys dressed up and tried to look solemn. Top are Bill Lytle, Steve Dugger, and Jim Hunt, bottom Ed Jeffries and Tom Taylor.

Stretch a rope knee-high, and you have a corral behind which horses will placidly, but interestedly, watch a little girl.

Every August Dalhart remembers its XIT days with a three-day Roundup. Most of the old hands are gone, but there are parades with lots of horses . . .

. . . pretty girls on floats, and Charlie Alford.

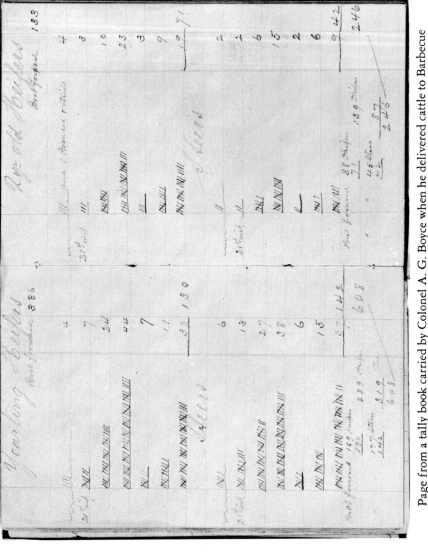

Page from a tally book carried by Colonel A. G. Boyce when he delivered cattle to Barbecue

"We were all silent for the longest minute I have ever lived. A million and one things went through my brain, and then I spoke up to Yearwood.

" 'You can send me,' I said, and before he could answer I blazed on, 'You said a man couldn't make the trip, and maybe you're right, but you didn't say anything about a boy. A boy could make it all right because they aren't going to think much about a young fellow going for evidence like that.'

" 'Cook, you're right. I believe that if anyone can make that trip you seem to have the right idea, and I know you have grit. Be here early in the morning and be ready to start,' Yearwood answered.

"Yearwood furnished me with a letter of credit from Mr. Findlay, purchasing agent of the XIT. He told me to show my letter at various ranches but to be careful with it. That little square piece of paper would be dynamite if the rustlers' friends were to get a hold of it.

"I started out in one of the durndest blizzards I've ever been in. The snow blinded me, and I had all I could do to keep my pony on the right road. We managed it somehow— it's pretty hard to throw a cowman off his trail, especially when his neck depends on his keeping it. The first place I stopped was the Cimarron Cattle Company. The manager was Colonel Crawford and I wanted to see him. He had his office in a little building to one side, and I tried over there. The snow had drifted knee-deep around the door and it seemed like it was getting colder all the time. I gave a good heavy knock, and a burly looking man opened the door a crack.

" 'What do you want?' he growled.

" 'Colonel Crawford,' I answered, and he slammed and barred the door.

"I waited a few minutes and then I knocked again. This

time the man seemed a little het up, but I knew it was my chance. I rammed my leg through the crack and forced it open. He cursed under his breath and I saw him put his hand on his gun.

"Colonel Crawford was sitting at a desk across the room, and I quickly went over to him. I gave him my letter and he called the man at the door and the other men in the room around him. I realized the seriousness of my situation more than ever. Those men were guarding Colonel Crawford against threats on his life, and for all they knew I might have been a rustler after his neck.

" 'He's all right, men,' Colonel Crawford said, and I felt a lot easier. They read and reread my letter, and then Colonel Crawford turned to me.

" 'You're on the right track all right, but tell me, are you the bravest son of a gun on the prairie or a fool? You're one or the other, or you wouldn't try this trip.'

" 'Fool,' I grinned. 'Only a fool would be caught out in this storm.'

" 'Do you know Jim Hisaw?' Crawford asked seriously.

" 'Is he a no-account, rotten, down-at-the-heel cut-throat, but a pretty good guy?' I asked.

" 'That's him,' Crawford answered. 'You see him for a horse at the line camp. The headquarters is alive with rustlers and it won't be very healthy for you there.'

"I followed my instructions and got my horse from Jim Hisaw. He was a likable cuss, and honest, except when business interfered.

" 'You're a native of this country, aren't you?' Jim asked. 'Well, you'll make it all right. There's nothing too hard for these darn Texans. They're the cussedest bunch of lawbreakers in the country, but the best souls that ever drew breath.' He was fixing my horse as he talked.

" 'If you ever want to pull a holdup, pard, come to Texas.

Go to Ranger; that little place has more outlaws than you can shake a stick at. Once my pardner and I was planning a T and P holdup and we needed one or two more good men. We pulled up to a saloon in Ranger, and I put the bartender next to what we wanted, and he promised to do all he could for us. The next day we met to rob the train, and I'll be a rat-eatin' chaparral if every darned man in town hadn't turned out to get a share of the loot. We held up the train all right, but my pard and I pulled out before we divided up. We knew there wouldn't be enough to go around.'

"He gave my saddle girth a last jerk and I was ready to leave.

"The next stop was Carbra Springs. It was Christmas Day, but I didn't have time to think of the fun the boys were having at the ranch. There was a little store that made up the town; so I had my Christmas dinner there. The storekeeper had a supply of canned goods and some crackers. I told him to give me a can of sardines, some peaches, and a box of crackers, and a knife to open the cans. He put them all on the table where I was sitting and I was about to open a can when he rammed his hand over mine.

" 'Not a bite until I see my money,' he said. I gave him a five-dollar bill, and I wish you could have seen him. 'Help yourself.' He told me to 'Open anything and everything in the whole store.'

"I changed horses at Carbra Springs, too. They were suspicious of me, and I didn't feel safe to show my letter. They asked a lot of questions and I had to think fast. They knew I was from the XIT, and then I told them I was making a trip to see about putting a telephone line through the country. One of them cursed and laughed, 'What'll them XIT guys be a-doing next?'

"I managed to get a horse by leaving my horse and thirty-five dollars in cash.

"After that I was over the border into New Mexico. I was pretty frozen and half-starved when I came to a camp of half-breed Mexicans. I wanted food for my horse and myself, but they claimed they had nothing. I knew their nature, so I gave them a dollar and they gave me a dinner of tortillas, beef, and coffee; and for another dollar they fed my horse.

"From there I made it to Las Vegas and to the ranch of the old Dutchman Huneke. Half of my trip was over. I had the evidence and now to get safely back to Alamositas.

"There was a half-breed Mexican that followed me around like a shadow. He wanted to go back with me and I was uneasy. Old man Huneke warned me that the Mexican's idea in going with me was to get rid of me. I made the Mexican ride in front and I warned him not to turn around. I knew I had to have him to recognize the horses the Rangers were holding that Arizona Johnny had stolen.

"I changed horses at the same places, and we got back to Alamositas in less time than it took to make the trip, although most of the trip was made across country without any roads.

"Mr. Findlay and Sheriff Robinson met me at Tascosa and they decided to send me with the Mexican to Vernon to identify the stolen horses.

"It was the last lap of the mile, and I knew my chances were too slim to meddle with, and I was determined that my trip to Las Vegas wouldn't be lost on the home stretch. When we got to Quanah I requested the Captain of the Rangers, MacDonald, to send a Ranger with me the rest of the way. He was glad to help me, and sent a man by the name of Tom Platt.

"The Mexican identified the horses as stolen and the men as the rustlers, and I must say it made me feel good all over to know that the state was rid of two of the criminals. Later I found out the men were sent to the penitentiary."

Such reminiscences as Cook's could go on and on, though

in less detail. Not all cowhands had the experience of being a teenage youth, new on the job, and traveling for evidence nearly seven hundred miles, half of it in a blizzard and the other half with a reluctant Mexican, through country whose people could be as cold and hostile as its climate. Rustling, says Haley, continued till the last steer was sold in 1912.

But though all of the 150 cowhands on the XIT at any given time might expect to go rustler-chasing, for most it would be a once-in-a-lifetime affair. And one, at least, refused to talk about it at all. That one is Gene Elliston, who avers as how he did "quite a bit of detective work . . . in the way of running down thieves, but as several of these characters are still living and some of them are trying to live straight now, I will not discuss these things—let bygones be bygones; may God bless them and help them to live a straight life."

Ira Aten's taste of rustling is more or less typical. A former Texas Ranger, he built a reputation for tracking stolen cattle while sheriff of Castro County, once returning more than three hundred head, plus the thieves, from the Washita River in Indian Territory. Over his wife's protest he resigned as sheriff to put his tracking experience to work for the XIT in 1895. With him he brought two comrades of Ranger days, Ed Connell and Wood Saunders. The trio oversaw four camps, stretching from the east to the New Mexico side of the ranch, beyond which lived a ruffianly group called by the cowboys "a hard formation."

There was some activity over the next several years, but Aten recalls, "finally it got too quiet for these daring old Rangers. They found no thrills in routine cowpunching and camp work, so they quit to hunt a new field." Chasing rustlers on the XIT was incidental to the job of being a hand; it was not a career in itself.

During the ten years he was Escarbada Division manager

Aten never had a man arrested. "What chance," he asked years later, "would a great cattle corporation have to convict a man of cattle stealing in Western Texas in those days? My time was too valuable to fool with the courts. Besides, arguments in court and grand juries often brought on a fight in which somebody was killed.

"When I left the ranch I turned it over to John Armstrong and gave him careful instructions how to handle the New Mexico cattle rustlers to put the fear of death into their hearts.

"Poor John, he was slack in his dealing with them and they killed him in about a year after I left."

Aten wasn't the only XIT man who had reason to believe that Panhandle courts didn't always punish the guilty or reward the innocent. Although it wasn't rustling that took him to court, an experience of H. S. Boice illustrates how Texas justice could be dispensed without regard to points of law.

After A. G. Boyce left the XIT, the syndicate tried to combine operation functions with ownership. Now Mexican hands insist that an owner cannot run a ranch unless it is too small to be called a ranch. If the XIT experience is any yardstick, the Mexican tradition is correct.

After the water supply was mismanaged—which means there wasn't any—the directors brought in H. S. Boice, who had traveled in Europe, was graduated from Princeton, had been president of the National Cattlemen's Association, and knew both culture and cows. He also said his prayers every night and was opposed to swearing.

Here Mrs. Duke picks up the narrative:

"Mr. Boice came on a man beating his horse over the head with a double of a rope, which can easily put out a horse's eye. Some said he was an outside man at a roundup in one of these western states. Mr. Boice interfered with 'abusive language,' the man said, which we do not believe, as no one ever accused Mr. Boice of abusive language at any other time or place. Then the man went after Mr. Boice with a knife and slashed him some. Result was a trial.

"The lawyer for the man knew his onions. He had heard that Mr. Boice said his prayers every night. Certainly, said Mr. Boice. The lawyer turned to the jury, 'Did you ever hear or know of a cowman that said his prayers any time?' They did not. Said the lawyer, 'All the evidence he has given is just as worthless as that.'

"Mr. Boice lost out and the jury decided that Mr. Boice was to be fined for interfering with the man in the controlling of his property; he was a meddler in another man's business."

Another case not designed to increase respect for juries was told to Mrs. Duke by her husband:

"One way of stealing cattle was to burn over the brand. The XIT brand was made with a bar about five inches long and five applications of the bar made this brand.

"Bob said of a man brought to trial that the jury acquitted him upon the ground that the conversion of the XIT brand into a lone star was an impossibility. All the lawyers on both sides of the case could not make a lone star of it. Now cow thieves are smart; the story honestly holds and they are aware of their constitutional guarantees against being held in jeopardy twice for the same offence.

"Once acquitted, the rustler took a piece of paper, called the jury around him, and with the pride of a craftsman, proceeded to show that it was not an impossibility; but to do so he had to search for cattle that had the brand with the stem of the 'T' slanting, as in branding if they did get the stem a-slanting they knew that it was a 'T' anyway."

Mrs. Duke continues: "Some rustlers kept stolen calves in a corral for a while, cut the muscles of their eyes so they drooped and they could not see when turned out. They bawled around for a few days and then hunted for food, but their eyelids always drooped a little.

"Another method employed by the rustlers was to burn the calves between the toes with a hot iron making their feet too sore for them to walk. A few rustlers would split their tongues so they could not nurse. Soon weaned, the rustler placed his own brand on them, a legally registered brand.

"When the brand did not show any too well that had been burned over, the animal killed, skinned, and on the wrong side of the hide, the first brand would show up the plainest.

"Once early in 1906 a young fellow had a claim over the state line in New Mexico. He intended to stay all summer, over six months as the law required him, then go back east to his old home and go to school. He did odd jobs of work and had come to the wagon where the boys had noticed his sallow complexion. He was another one who had come to the plains, the high altitude country that cured chills and fever, or malaria.

"This boy had noticed the fences, their wires cut from one line-rider's day to another. Of course the line rider would not make the round again for several days. He had also noticed some gentry who seemed well-heeled, did not work, and slept most of the day.

"It is the same in all times and countries. There are people who never work, do not have much property and as the law says 'Have no visible means of support.' Yet these people seemed to do very well and had good horses. There is something crooked about it all. At that time all the people raised cattle or row crops for cattle. They were concerned with cattle one way or another. These people were, too.

"This boy when he came to the wagon told of some curious things going on. Some of these scalawags had tried to get him to join them with the same old argument: 'The big feller

running over the little feller.' He did not join them; he was
not raised that way, he said.

"One evening two men rode up to his shack, a half-dug-
out, and called him out. They told him that if he did not
leave the country in twenty-four hours they would kill him.
The men were both armed with guns, two big men to see a
boy not well, but that is always the calibre of this kind of
men.

"After they had issued orders, the boy went back into the
dugout and at once reappeared with his shotgun, and shooting, too. He filled one man's arm with shot and peppered the
other. They loped off, one of them saying he was killed. The
two went to a doctor and told a great tale of what happened
to them. The boy left the country that night and Bob did not
know where he went to, as Bob paid him in cash for work
and information.

"Not so long after this happening Bob got into trouble
with cattle thieves at Endee, New Mexico, a post office and
general store just over the line from the XIT. After Ira Aten
left the Escarbada Division, south of Endee, thieves still
abounded. This was in 1906 but in December, 1905, Bob had
been given charge of all the territory north of the Canadian
River. The pasture Minneosa was mostly north of the river,
but there was a big stretch of it south of the river, and he had
all of it in his charge.

"Camp Trujillo was at the south end of Minneosa and not
far from Endee, New Mexico. This Minneosa Pasture faced
New Mexico, for the whole of Oldham County in Texas. As
it was on both sides of the Canadian River, it was a great
place of hills, draws, canyons, trees, and running water. It
was a good breeding range and also a good range for cattle
thieves. Along the Canadian over in New Mexico the cattle
could be hid very easily, where there was plenty of running

water. But the thieves had gotten careless; they had been stealing as many as twenty-five head at once and taking them out on the flats where they could graze. However, when Bob took charge, they moved a lot of black-polled cattle in where Herefords and Shorthorns had been before.

"The two cowboys or line riders at Trujillo Camp wore guns. They had heavy shades at the windows of their camp. These cowboys rode the west line of fence every day.

"Endee, just across the line from Texas and south of Trujillo, had a dwelling house which contained a small grocery store, a postoffice, and a few extra rooms to rent to people who came along. These travelers had been few and far between, but this year of 1906 their trade was picking up, as people were coming in and buying land for farming.

"The year before 1905 was a very wet year, a year of excessive rain. Even the chuck wagon could not move with the cow outfit. The cowboys had to put everything on pack horses. As one cowboy remarked, 'a horse sunk to the hock joint out on the prairie sod.'

"One of the boys from the chuck wagon would go to Endee once a week to get the mail. Now a certain cowboy had become acquainted with the daughter of the Endee postman. In fact they were becoming sweethearts. This cowboy would tell the girl what a good fellow Duke was as a boss; that he always led in the work, saw that they had the best of food, a good cook, and a prompt pay check every month. This boy was hoping to get married and still work for Duke. Some cowboys had married and lived in permanent camps in the past.

"Bob had come to Endee this time to stay all night as he was on his way to Escarbada to see C. R. Smith, who was leaving August 1 to go into the land business at Hereford. There was no railroad there yet, but the railroad was built through Endee in 1909. There was no place in miles for Bob

to stay. He could not take his bedroll with him, so he had to
go to Endee to stay all night.

"When he had gotten a room for the night, the daughter
followed him in and told him that she had overheard two
men who had been waiting there for him, and intended to
kill him. They were going to get into a poker game in the
dining room, get into a scuffle and in it would shoot him.
They were told that he did not play cards. Very well, they
would get into an argument over poker and in the scuffle in
the hall would break his door down and shoot him, claiming
self defense or any old defense.

"At supper that evening across the table from Bob sat a
man and a woman, who in collusion had raided upon Texas
brands, to get cattle into New Mexico. At each end of the
table sat one of these men who had conspired to kill him.

"The talk at the table was all about the selling of land and
how many buyers were going in to settle up the country. The
land was cheap to them and such crops as they had raised the
year before was what they wanted. One of Aten's Rangers
had come back, Connell, and was taking a Wright Land
Company man into the Escarbada near there. It looked like
the XIT would soon all go to farming.

"Talk of new buyers led around to Bob. Would Duke
farm?

" 'Me? No. I've been here eleven years and there have been
more dry than wet years in that time. It is easier to take cattle
to water than water to crops.'

" 'Yes,' cut in some one, 'the cattle market is so rotten.'

" 'That is so,' said Bob.

"Bob believed this girl, and why? It was because her boy
friend was a great worker and so was she.

"Why did these men want to kill him? Well, as long as
Ira Aten was there Bob did not do much about cattle rustling;
he let Ira Aten and his two Texas Rangers, Connell and

Saunders, do that. But now here was something for him to do. The cattle rustlers thought that they had plain sailing, now that Ira Aten was gone.

"That spring of 1906 they had been putting telephones in all over the ranch so that camps and headquarters could be reached at once, especially in case of fire. Ira Aten had found his fences torn down and cows and calves taken out. He had armed his cowboys and went after them in New Mexico, and always rounded them up and got them home before the thieves could brand the calves.

"Now this work would be thrust on Bob. The one rider had been shot at and run off. The fence had been torn down for a quarter of a mile and about fifty cows with their calves had been driven out of the XIT Ranch into New Mexico. The line rider got to the nearest telephone, and as the wagon was in the north end of Minneosa rounding up dry cows to ship in June, the wagon and Bob got there that same day to Camp Trujillo.

"Bob armed all of his outfit with revolvers, shotguns, and rifles, and away they went following the trail. They came up to this herd of cows and calves. It was very easy to come up to them; they were the only black-polled cattle in the country. As they came up to the herd, which was being driven by three men, two of the men 'lit out' for parts unknown. The herd had been going very slowly because the calves were small. Now the other man was a newcomer and didn't know much about the country. Bob rode up to him.

" 'These are our cattle, the only X-branded black cattle in the country. Look at our horses, all of them with XIT branded on the hip. We are taking these cattle back, and don't you make a move to stop us or it will go hard with you,' said Bob. He went on, 'You can tell the gentlemen that rode off that anyone found inside the XIT fence and not working for the XIT outfit will be shot at. If necessary, we will get Rangers to watch that line fence.'

"And so they found that they had another Ira Aten. So they would get rid of him. These two men at the table were the two men that had left the herd, and had 'lit out.'

"Some time later the boy told Bob that the two men did break the door down and then shoot around, but found nobody. The two or three land men there made a big fuss over it. They said that they would not stop there any more; that they would take their camp equipment along with them and camp out on the prairie if that happened again. They would let other real estate men know about it. Settlers would not come into a country where the citizens shot up the home of the storekeeper and the postman.

"But soon the XIT company moved all cows and calves out of Minneosa and put steers in the pasture, as they were much easier to move off the land when it was sold. These rustlers did not steal steers, as the brand on them had grown so that they could not change it. They had no more trouble with cattle rustlers in Minneosa after it was closed out as a breeding range."

One last note on rustling should be added, more for its syntax than for any informational contribution. When in 1893 the XIT introduced the first black muley cattle into the area, rustlers would steal in from across the New Mexico border by night and take the black calves. "They got a start and that was enough for them," comments Mrs. Duke.

Three of the New Mexicans, according to W. T. Brown, who was in Channing at the time, crossed over to kill A. G. Boyce. That they didn't succeed is evident from Boyce's continuing to live rather than from Brown's story, the lines of which get a little tangled:

"They were cattle thieves and dreaded Mr. Boyce, but Mr.

Boyce was at the Yellow Houses Division. They closed up the town and wired Tascosa for John King, sheriff, and Johnny Brofa, deputy. They come and had a fight with them. They shot two of them and took them to the Tascosa jail. These men were not afraid of anything and went out after any bad men."

So the XIT stayed out of the courthouse if at all possible and took direct action in its own behalf. It had hundreds of miles of open border that invited the greedy to slip in, but its men were vigilant and devoted, if not always impregnable. To the last, it is agreed, defense against rustling was the problem that required the most attention and returned the least reward.

"Of all the horses I ever forked—"

HORSES

"MUCH ADO is made nowadays about rodeos. Why, in the roundup season of the year we had one every day after dinner. Each man had two good broke horses in his mount, and after dinner was the time to ride them. Some six or eight men would ride their broncs all at once—a regular six-ring circus, and such pitching and bucking you never saw before. People would come from afar to see our rodeos."

It wasn't all a horse circus by any means. But the cowboy is famed as the knight on horseback, and the XIT hand was no exception. He had to know how to sit a horse, to take care of a horse, to work from a horse, in effect to live with a horse. When the old XIT hands gather for their yearly reunion in

Dalhart each August, some of their tenderest, and some of their wildest, memories stem from their associations with horses.

The XIT had good horses. At first the ranch imported its mounts from South Texas. Mainly they were older Spanish horses with outsize Mexican brands all over their hips; some were "gotch-eared, mostly red roans and gruyers, some fine old cowhorses and some spoilt outlaws."

After the XIT had begun to raise its own horses, every colt, like every calf, was branded on its jaw with the year of its birth. As the horse matured it was watched closely, and when it began to show age it was retired, or "condemned," as one hand put it. Men were assigned regular bronco-busting chores, and after they had ridden wild horses a few times, the "half-broke" horses were added to the various cowboys' strings. By fall they were usually well broken. After that, with the hardest riding behind for the year, the cowboy turned out all his string except two or three favorites for his winter mount.

Occasionally a hand lost his mount. North of the Platte in Wyoming, Milt Whipple, a trail boss, lost an old dun that he used as a night horse. All spring and summer he looked for him, and wondered. In the fall Whipple went back up the trail, but still no dun. When in the next spring Whipple's outfit began gathering saddle horses at Rito Blanco, the boss decided to make a drive down into the breaks where the old dun had usually wintered in the past. There the horse was, on his old range. By himself he had come all the way from Wyoming.

Horses' names ran the gamut from commonplace, to literary, to imaginative. J. W. Standifer's winter mount consisted of Limber Jim and Spike, "two of the finest cutting horses I ever rode." Lynn Boyce's favorite horse was Rooster, a sorrel paint. Another hand chose Trilby and Terrapin for his winter mount, while Roy Frye claimed Sop an' Taters as part of his string.

A horse might well be the cowman's best friend, and his most understanding working partner. Another horse might be the death of him. But whatever the quality or whatever the disposition of the cowboy's mount, his horse was the one piece of equipment he found absolutely indispensable. The horse was a working tool, a means of transportation, and sometimes the difference between survival and death.

Almost invariably the horse came first, and many a cowboy carried a can of tomatoes for his horse when he rode into the alkali lake country. The cowboy drank the alkali water straight, but the horse had his with tomatoes.

One mistake that so many painters of Western scenes have made consistently is to depict whole herds as if all horses in those herds possessed the same emotions and reactions. Like human beings, horses have individuality, and to lump them together as if their instincts and behaviors were all the same is as foolish as to suggest that all Texans are tall, or garrulous, or hard-drinking. Each horse represented a separate problem, and every hand found greater success working with some horses than he did with others.

Gene Elliston, for instance, found a horse he could neither ride nor walk:

"I ask for a horse to take Bob East's horse back to him at Channing. He said go back to the ranch and tell the man there to let me have a horse by the name of Old Frank. He got the word all right. He was a skuball [skewbald], stocking-legged, knock-kneed, hipped horse. He was locoed, would not lead—so I rode him and led Bob's horse back to Channing. Next morning early Frank and myself started for the ranch. We carapated* thoroughly until Frank got hot.

* Capered. The action of some horses when first mounted is a kind of prancing, or dancing, called "capering."

I did not have any spurs or rope; my bridle reins were short. I was just a product of Jack County in my teens. However I had been pretty well raised on a horse but the calves chewed my bridle reins up before I left home and I had lost my spurs, and as I said Frank was locoed and would not lead. I thought of walking but he would not lead; so it was up to me to do the caraparating [capering]. I could not find any switches—I was too far from Jack County now—but I could tell by the sun I was making progress. We got into the Ojo Bravo Ranch before sunrise next morning. Frank had not been on such a long journey for twenty years. Of all the horses I ever forked* he was the sorriest."

Almost every ranch had one or more outlaw horses, broncos "as bad as ever wore hair." One of the XIT outlaws was named Rosy Brown, "a slim, smooth, blood bay, a beautiful horse, but with wicked ways." According to Worth Jennings, only one hand could ever ride him—a cowboy named Anderson Witherspoon, would ask for Rosy Brown from choice. But Anderson, says Jennings, could ride anything.

"Many times I have seen some poor boy standing, shaking in his boots after every one had mounted and Anderson would say, 'Want me to top him for you?' And he would."

It was a bit rougher going for J. A. Smiley, who looked back over a half-century to recount some of his riding experiences:

"That spring while we were breaking broncs we had a rodeo every day. We didn't have to have a chute to put them in, then crawl on top of the chute to get on the bronc, we just roped him in the corral and saddled him. When we got six or seven saddled we would open up the big gate and turn them down the flat. South of the flat, then the show would

* Mounted.

start; some of them would pitch and some would just run. Some people think that all broncs are bad pitchers, but that is a mistake. There is about one in ten that can do the real thing. When you find one that can go high and come down with his head where his tail was, you had better have your riding clothes on when you get on him. When you find a blue dun with stripes around his legs and a dark stripe down his back with the brand JB on his left shoulder and fire in his eyes, you had better divide your money, and put half of it in each pocket, then part your hair in the middle and get your earthly business all fixed up before you get on him, for a strawberry roan isn't in it to the side of old JB.

"After we got back home and rested up and let our horses rest up, we rounded up the little beef pasture that day I rode Old D Grey. He was a good cutting horse, but he was like I am now—he had just been here too long. There was a few cows and heifers had got in with the steers; so we had to cut them out. I rode out about the middle of the roundup. I found a line-back ringey-tailed heifer. When I turned Old D in after her and started her toward the outside of the roundup, Old D commenced to get busy. When he got her out she turned down the edge of the roundup and Old D began to stumble, and [I] thought he was going to fall. So I just went off of him like a bat out of a well and just skinned nearly all the hide off of my hands and knees. But Old D didn't fall. So I got up bloody as a stuck hog and got on Old D and brought her out to the cut next time. So we got the herd started for the general beef pasture on the South Canadian River.

"The second day at noon we taken . . . at the east end of [Spring] Lake. Now there is where I rode the black bronc again. We rounded up the horses; I saddled the black bronc. As soon as I hit the saddle he went in the air. I was just a little bit out of humor. Anyway, I had a little misunderstanding that day with one of the waddies and I was craving a little excitement, and right there I got plenty of it. I reached up in his shoulders with a pair of petmakers* and he showed me how quick he could turn in the air and how high he could go before he come down. He didn't give me time to think between times, but he give me the benefit of a reasonable doubt when he lit and started to run. Fortunately he started northwest up the trail the way we was going. I begin to think that I was going to win. He would run a while and pitch a while. After he went about four miles he give out.

"One of the boys overtook the horse wrangler roundup and got me another horse. So things was pretty good for a day or so. Finally one day we was moseying along when Joe Ford's horse come by with one of his boots in the stirrup. Well, we thought Joe was either killed or all broke up. We caught Joe's horse and taken back, we found old Joe up on his pins. His horse had fell and knocked him out—mashed up his ankle a little. He was crippled for a few days, but old Joe was too tough to stay crippled long at a time; he was a little man but he could 'ear down' the biggest bronc on the range. While me and old Rube Burnett put the kack on him, we got up about No. 4 Division. They had a No. 7 bronc there. All of our horses was branded XIT on the hip but each division number was branded on the neck. Ours was No. 7; so they wasn't allowed to ride a No. 7 horse.

"We camped there that night; so the next morning they turned the bronc over to us. He was dun with stripes around his legs and a stripe down his back, and he was fat. So Uncle Henry said to me, 'John, you are the heftiest man in the outfit, so you can have the extra dun.' I roped him, old Joe eared him down, I threw my kacktus on him, and I went on him. He showed me tricks he had learned down Red River. He had been rode before and spoiled, probably had spilled a

* Spurs.

waddie or two. He went plenty high and he was plenty fast, but he performed on a small space of ground but he didn't have the wind to stay in the game like the black. After it was all over, and I had got back to normal, Uncle Henry said, 'Well boys, that's the worst one we've had,' but I knew better—the black bled me. I spit up blood the next morning after I rode him. I named the dun Mack. He never pitched anymore. He was lame in one shoulder as long as I rode him.''

Alec Sevier's recollections of horses are mixed. Here are some of them:

"I met Bob as we rode around the herd. He says, 'Alec, do you know where the wagon is?' I told him I thought I did as I could see a windmill every time it lightninged. He says, 'That may be Big Well on a hill to the north of us about four miles.' I told him I did not think the herd had run far, as they had been milling most of the time. He told me to try to find it and wake up the other boys. So I rode off in the direction I thought it was, and rode until I knew, or thought, I was past it. So I stopped and waited a while and decided to go back to the herd and take another start. I was riding a brown horse named Gyp. I did not have much faith in him as a night horse, but he proved true that time. I was riding in a slow walk back toward the herd and he stopped stock still. I sat there and waited for a flash of lightning, which was less frequent. When the flash came Old Gyp had his head right over the potrack not ten feet from the back end of the wagon.

"Boy, howdy, I fell in love with old Gyp right there. I woke the boys and went back to the herd and stayed an hour or two. Bob told me to go to the wagon and get some sleep. I went, but not to sleep. It had started to rain again and I did not want to unroll again. So I crawled in the wagon, but it was not a very good bedground.

"A while before day one of the other boys came to the wagon and I asked him how the herd was doing. He said they were still walking but had not run any more. I asked him what he come in for; he said he was hungry. I says, 'Do you expect to find anything to eat this early in the day?' He said, 'You bet!' and filled his coat pockets full of prunes and went back to the herd.

"The next morning the horses were all gone and the first drag for them netted everybody a horse except Bob Duke. Some of the boys offered to lend him one. He said, 'No, I'll ride Red Cloud.' He was the horse that wore the bell and didn't anybody ride. Bob roped him, saddled him, and stepped on him. He went to bucking and that old big bell would go round and round his neck. When he quit Bob got off him. He said he wouldn't ride a horse that couldn't pitch any higher than that. 'I'll just tie him here and wait for a gentle one.' Bob was a fine rider and it took a powerful horse to interest him much.

"We turned this herd loose on the Buffalo Springs range and went back to Rito Blanco to put the hay up. This was the year the management decided to throw Middle Water and Rito Blanco together, with Bob Duke as boss, but Bob wouldn't take the job. So they sent to Bovina for President Abbott to take charge. Then they rounded up the Rito Blanco horses and let the Buffalo Springs and Middle Water boys top them to suit themselves, and you can guess how that suited the Rito Blanco lads—by the last of September they were all gone. We all went to the Prairie Cattle Company.

"One day I was riding Slim Jim, a big heavy brown horse and as treacherous as he was good. I was dragging hides out to where the freight wagons could get to them. I had one hide tied on my rope and got down to tie another and old Jim got to raising hell—got tangled up in the rope and went to pitching and kicking. I had hold of the bridle reins when the show started, and we had it around and around, but he finally jerked loose from me and left there with that cowhide tied to him. I followed him about two miles and piled my spurs, six gun, and coat upon a hill where I could find them the next day and walked on. I got to the Rito Blanco gate on the E Road. Old Jim had been there and turned south to a drop gap east of Bouldin Dam. I waited and watched down the fence, and pretty soon I saw old Jim top a divide coming back in a lope.

"I sat down and waited for him. When he saw me he began to neigh and came right up to me. I reached up and took the rope off the saddle horn and cut a pair of bridle reins off it. He had stepped on the leather reins and broke them off until they were too short to ride with. I got my outfit fixed up, went and opened the gate, went back to Jim, caught the bridle reins, and told him to come on. He had not moved out of his tracks. The old cuss had had enough running for one time. That old hide laid around the gate for years but you bet not many people knew how come it was there, for I never told a soul about that for years."

Standifer had as his regular mounts Big Sunday, Bluedog, Wheeler, Spanish, Buck, Boots—his night horse—and Lina, a big black, "very high strung and snorty." When a camp of travelers crossing the XIT let their horses get away they sent a boy to the ranch to borrow a horse for searching. Standifer sent Lina.

When the boy returned, Standifer asked him how he liked Lina.

"I liked him fine, but he sure flung papa, and as papa was a preacher, I don't guess he liked him so well."

Bob Dudley, who "often wondered why . . . cowboys could be thrown . . . without . . . being seriously injured," liked to take on a wild cow now and then. He seems to have been thrown indiscriminately by both equine and bovine types.

"Rito Blanco Division had as good horses to ride as any ranch in the state of Texas, and plenty of them," Dudley writes. "I had eleven horses in my string there. When I first began work on Rito Blanco in 1893 Mr. Eubank issued me ten horses, and after about a month he told me he had an extra horse that was fat as butter which had been rode very little, as he was rather draggy and very difficult to mount. He said I could have this extra if I wanted him, and I promptly accepted the horse and found he was living up to his reputation both as to laziness and to being mean to get on. He eventually became full of pep and made a very good horse, and I was still riding him when I quit Rito Blanco in 1896. We always had a number of pitching horses on the ranch, as well as a lot of gentle ones also.

"There was a time when I was thrown twice a year on an average, but with age and experience I improved some in riding, as well as other parts of the cow work. I rode from November, 1891, to September, 1895, without getting thrown, and then was thrown in half the time it takes to say 'Jack Robinson' with your mouth already open for the start. Had rode that horse as his turn came from May to September, and very few rides had he failed to try to throw me and pitched eight different times with me in one afternoon. It being a rainy afternoon and wearing a slicker caused the extra number of trials. I knew all the time he could throw me, but this particular time he just wanted to show how quickly he could do the job.

"Perhaps you've often heard someone say that so-and-so is such a good rider that no horse could throw him. My advice is don't take such a statement too seriously. In other words, when you hear of someone who can not be thrown, well, just don't let it sink in too deep, as anyone with years and years of experience on the old-time 'big ranches' knows someone is sadly mistaken. True, some riders are very difficult to throw off, but it can be did at some time and in some way. In the summer of 1899 it came my time for another spill, or as cowboys used to say 'stake another claim.'

"This time I had lost a silver-mounted spur, and the horse was too long-winded for me with only one spur. I could not sit there any longer.

"Some of us used to when dehorning old or off-colored cows get quite a thrill by stepping astride the cow while she was still on the ground and when she got up we would be already mounted for a ride back to the other cattle on the other side of the corral, and then jump off. They would invariably do more or less bucking and sometimes a lot of bellowing also, as each ride was the cow's first and only experience.

"Enough about riding XIT cows, but why not try it sometime yourself? On a really wild cow, not a tame one. It's real fun to feel the cow's hide roll back and forth with each jump they make and feel the quiver of the body each time they try to bellow more loudly and excitedly than the time before."

As is well known, cowboy humor was about as subtle as cowboy speech. No form of humor could bring as much pure, simple joy to a group of cowmen as the practical joke. Probably no joke was as side-splittingly hilarious as enticing some tenderfoot aboard the "hurricane deck" of a bad horse—as entertainment it belonged in the same category as watching your best friend fall down a flight of stairs.

When W. A. Askew was new to the XIT, he was lured into saddling a gentle antique called "Old Nigger." Askew had no sooner mounted than—

"Old Nigger swallowed his tail and away he went. I was hanging on for dear life and using all I knew about riding a bad horse. The old horse pitched for an hour but I stayed up there, and the boys laughed and cried and rolled in the grass and there was nothing so funny as getting a tenderfoot on a bad horse.

"When I got down I was bleeding at the nose, my eyes were black, my head was aching, and I was practically a wreck, but when we had a new man come to camp I was in for him to ride Old Nigger, and from that time I rode Old Nigger until I left the ranch, but I never saw a cowboy but what he would throw sometime. Of course these boys thought I was a tenderfoot, but I had rode the range with Uncle Charlie Goodnight."

Scottie was a Swede who had come to the United States as a valet for John Farwell. Somehow he became a ranch hand for a short time, in which capacity "he got the little end of all the jokes and lies." Educated, he could speak several languages and "cuss fluently in all of them." Naturally enough, the boys gave him a barely broken horse named The Colt. Scottie never clambered aboard without coming back down faster, and the boys never tired of Scottie's "variety of cussing."

Another tenderfoot was Steve Dugger, who arrived at Farwell Park, or Perico, to work for the XIT. When R. L. Duke asked him whether he could ride, Dugger told him frankly that he was "not so very good." Duke decided to test him with a horse named Spuds.

"I didn't know much about bad horses, as I had just come off the farm. I took him out to saddle him. I did not get my saddle on him before he broke loose and ran away from me. Florence Moore, the wagon boss, told me to let him go, they would catch me another. I got the saddle on this horse and made it very well.

"They was taking a herd to Buffalo Springs. We got there that night, turned the herd loose. The wagon boss caught me a night horse the next morning, which was something new to me. I got up and wrestled horses the next morning, and when I got back they had all eat breakfast. I went to the wagon to eat, looked out toward the horses, and they had a horse caught by the name of 'Sport.' Two cowboys were holding his head, another putting my saddle on him. I got so excited I could not eat. I went out and asked Mr. Moore if he was going to have me ride that horse. He told me I hired out to be a cowboy and they had these horses to ride, and if I couldn't do it there was a man living in town on a cracker a day that could. I told him I was just as near broke as that man was and if he could do that job, then I could too. They had him saddled by that time and I had got over my scare and was about half mad. I told them to hold him until I could get on him. I pulled down my hat and says to the boys, 'I'll ride that horse or pull that saddle horn off or my arm one.'

"I got upon him and I told them to turn him loose. He seemed to me like he joined the birds in the air but I was lucky enough to stay with him. The boys all whooping and hollering says 'Stay with him, farmer boy.' They thought if I could ride that horse I might make a cowboy. Then they started giving me bad horses. Some was worse than that horse.

"I'd get throwed about two or three times a day. I was skinned all over. I made up my mind I was going to stay with it, as I didn't want anyone living on a cracker a day doing something I couldn't do."

Another time Dugger was out with a horse herd of 150 head when, who knows for what reason, the herd stampeded.

"I was trying to circle them, not knowing where I was. I ran over the XIT fence, which had some ribbon wire on it. My horse fell over this fence, I fell off and held to the bridle reins. He got up bucking and raising Cain. I was trying to hold him but he pushed me back through the fence. The wire cut one of my chap legs off but he didn't hurt me. So I had to turn him loose; he just got away from me, and the horses got away.

"This other cowboy found me and neither of us knew where we was. We stayed in the snowstorm all night and I had lost my hat, was bareheaded. To keep from freezing to death, I trotted in a circle all night long. This other cowboy was somewhat older than I. He would give out and try to sit down beside a soapweed or yucca. I would tell him if he sat there he would freeze to death and he said he was give out, but I told him he had to keep moving. We made out until daylight, we both got on his horse and started to find the wagon. We run on to my horse and saddle. He was so badly cut up with the wire that he could not move. I took my saddle off him and throwed it down on the prairie and went on to find the wagon. I told them what had happened.

"The other boys started out to gathering the horses over the range. I got back to Mr. Moore's wagon that night. He told me I would be on horse wrestle the next night, so caught me another night horse. He gave me a horse that was as bad as the horse called 'Sport.' I rode back up to Mr. Moore and told him if he had any more outlaws for night horses, I would like to try them out before dark."

The first XIT horse that Earl Davis rode surprised him by refusing to move at all. While Davis saddled him, Old Louis stood stockstill. Davis climbed up, "and he still stood still. So I kicked him in the ribs, and, say, he moved that time."

"He bucked down south, then east, then north, and when he got back to the barn he stopped—but I didn't. I went on through the barn and busted two 1 x 12 boards. I got up, and, say, I was mad. I wanted to fight everybody for jobbing me. But all they could do was to laugh. Then I took it out on Louis. It was against the rules to spur a horse in the shoulder, but Louis got lots of it.

"I rode the condemned horse called Curlew. This horse

killed a man, fell backwards with him. I had no trouble. I
had to start the horse off in a trot and jump on him while
trotting."

One night in the Capitol Pasture, according to S. R.
Cooper, a big sorrel broke away, only to be roped. With two
men hanging on to the rope, he ran about three miles before
catching a herd of mustangs, where he broke free. About two
weeks later the sorrel returned to the remuda in the night.
Once again the twine was put on him, and three men held
him while another saddled and helped the rider up.

"The horse got his nose between his knees, and a hump on
his back like a camel, and bawling like a cow lost from her
calf, and as he came alongside a water trough and water had
wasted out some and the ground muddy and slick, and down
he came broadside, but his rider lit on his feet and held the
reins and when the horse got to his feet again he seemed to be
over his frolic and the rider went into the saddle again and
rode off like you would an old plow mule.

"One Sunday when I was at the ranch I got on one of the
two-year-olds, but he was so stubborn I couldn't get him
very far from the pens, and the boy and another man that
had just come there to get a job was going to Soda Lake for a
swim. So the new man saddled up a fresh horse and I rode
the boy's private horse and the boy rode the three-year-old
mustang. We made it all O.K. going to the lake, and after
we played in the water as long as we wanted we started back
to the ranch, and this new man bantered me for a race and as
the land was smooth and level it was a fine place to try them
out and the horses were feeling good, but we had not run far
when his horse got a little ahead so I used my bridle reins to
encourage my horse, but he either did not understand what I
meant or became offended, for he dropped his head—and
also me—and as I hit that smooth prairie I hardly knew when
to quit rolling, and when I came to my feet again, I was the

drunkest I ever was in my life. The other two boys came to me and asked me if I was hurt and when they found out I was all O.K. we all had a good laugh and I topped my horse again and returned to the ranch."

J. W. Standifer writes of a different kind of riding— *behind*, not *on*, as he and others drove wagons.

"One fall I worked Jennie and Katie, a little pair of mare mules that were possessed with the devil. About a dozen times a day Katie would kick one leg over the tongue. Then they would pretend to be scared, and away they would run like scared jackrabbits. Lots of times I have pulled the whole weight of the buckboard with the reins, for miles at a time.

"Part of the winter we had a big white horse and spring wagon, sent out from town to feed in. His name was Buckshay. He had a crippled foot and had to wear a special-made shoe. But it didn't slacken his gait any. He was the friskiest old devil I ever saw. All he had to do all day was haul a few sacks of cake about a mile, and he ate two big feeds of chops a day. So it was small wonder that I often wished for an anchor to drag behind that wagon when I headed homeward on a frosty morning.

"Bob Hunt drove six big horses to his chuck wagon, ever one of them as black as a crow. And when he'd pop his whip over their backs, and they began to prance, they made a never-to-be-forgotten picture. Their names were Hawk and Rep, Nigger and Curley, Midnight and Henry. They told it on him that one time a lady asked how many courses he had. He thought she said horses, so he answered six. The lady was surprised that cowboys served meals in six courses, so she asked him to name them, and he obediently named his six black horses for her. And added 'there ain't a better team in all Texas either.'

"They sure did have a fine bunch of horses, the best as a whole that I ever saw on one ranch. The company had quit raising their own colts several years before, but they still had a surplus of unbroken horses. These horses were all broke to stand wherever you let the reins fall, even the wilder ones never left their riders afoot. But no matter how gentle a horse became he could never be caught without being roped. This was always the wagon boss's job and it took a good roper to do it too. The horses soon learned to hide and dodge; they got the art down pretty fine. Each called out which horse he wanted to ride. They usually changed several times a day when possible.

"It was a pretty and interesting sight to watch the horse wrangler bring in the remuda and see them go in their corral made only of one rope stretched about four feet high— any of them could have easily jumped, but they never did— and the older horses that had had lots of experience would make for the outside circle and brace themselves with their forefeet so the inside ones wouldn't push them over the rope. Every cowboy always laid his saddle a certain way and spread his blanket so the sweat would dry. In later years none of the horses had sore backs. They had improved so in making saddles that it took a mean horse master to hurt his horse's back."

On the way to Cheyenne once Standifer received a surprise he never forgot. He and another cowboy had orders to cross the Canadian River, "and at this point it was a treacherous stream. About one hundred yards wide, filled with quicksand. We were both scared to death, but orders were orders. So we took a running start and busted her wide open. We imagined it was four or five feet deep with a quicksand bottom. And were surprised to find it only about knee-deep with a solid bed."

One man whose feats with horses were legendary, even among men who looked on superior horse-handling as routine, was Uncle Jack Leonard, who, like Standifer, had his best experiences from behind a horse—or rather, teams of horses. Edward MacConnell tells about him:

"I first saw old Uncle Jack on the Rito Blanco when he pulled out to let Mike [Henry Michaels] and I have half of the road of our windmill outfit, which was being pulled by Belle and Marge. The sight of Belle and Marge (you remember Belle—she was the hellion) recalled to Jack's mind the time he was using them as leaders in a six-horse team on a wagon and trailer to haul some ties up near Romero.

"Jack said he was stuck and had been working to get his loads out of the sand for some time without success. The team just could not pull the heavy wagons loaded as they were; so Jack decided to throw off some of the ties, but first got down and started up toward his leaders with the intention of making some adjustment in the harness. Just then a Rock Island engine whistled, and between chuckles, Jack said 'and damned if old Belle and Marge didn't sink into them collars and run off with the whole damn outfit, mules, wagon, and all.'

"Those of you who remember the size of this cantankerous span of bay mules will not doubt Jack's veracity. But the story I like best about this old man is the one told to me by Mike, regarding an incident which took place at the cap rock between Channing and Rito Blanco.

"Hall Medford and Uncle Jack, with six horses or mules and two wagons each, were freighting cottonseed cake to Rito Blanco on a cold snowy day. About two inches of snow lay on the level, and the trail down the cap rock had filled with a number of drifts. Hall was in the lead and stopped at the summit to wait for Jack, from whom he borrowed additional chains with which to lock all four wheels on both his wagons, as he deemed the going too rough and dangerous to permit rolling wheels.

"Jack tossed him down the chains and then sat up on his

front load and, without comment, watched Hall get everything snug and secure and wind slowly down to the bottom
of the arroyo, where he took off the chains and, holding them
up, yelled, 'I'll have 'em right back up, Uncle Jack.'

"Jack reared up on his hind legs and yelled, 'Get the hell
out of the way. I'm coming down.'

"With a Comanche yell he set his team into the collars on
the run and, with one foot on the brake and the other braced
on the load, his long gray hair flowing in the breeze, the old
man took those six mules and two wagons around the turns
and down to the bottom almost before Hall, despite his fran-
tic haste, could get out of his way."

Chillcut's favorite riding horse was Skeeter. The first several times they went out together Skeeter would set his forefeet and stop cold whenever he saw a cow on the prairie, and
Chillcut would sail over his head. As soon as Chillcut caught
on, Skeeter never threw him again. Except for this one
idiosyncracy, Skeeter responded perfectly, and Chillcut cannot remember ever using spurs on him.

One day Tom Taylor bet a group of hands that he could
ride Cowboy, his favorite bay, after the horses without saddle
or bridle. Everyone within calling distance stopped work to
come watch. For a hundred yards Taylor was correct, but for
no discernible reason Cowboy "decided he didn't want to
leave the barn, and when his lord and master tried to make
him, he downed his head and threw him high, wide, and
handsome."

For a long time Tom Dixon was a bog rider, with three
horses—Wagon, Snip, and Bib Cody—in his string. "I will
never forget those faithful horses and can still see them in
my mind," he wrote years later. With Dixon rode a hand
named Bob, whose pet horse was Monkey Face. "He rode
him in the winter and also in the spring work. Monkey Face
had a habit of breaking in two and every once in a while he

threw Bob, but he loved him more than any horse he had."

It could almost be added that most of the cowboys on the XIT could paraphrase that statement and say, with Tom Dixon, that they each had a horse that they loved more than any human being they ever knew. Horse and man might be a little brutal in their treatment of each other when they first met, but once they understood their mutual relationship, they worked together in a harmony that few human beings ever achieve with each other.

This harmony was natural, but if it had not been, it would have been an enforced relationship. Shortly after he became general manager in the 1880's Colonel Boyce got together with George Findlay to draft a code of rules for the ranch. The most famous regulation, and most stringently enforced, was Rule No. 9, as follows:

"The abuse of horses, mules, or cattle by an employee will not be tolerated; and anyone who strikes his horse or mule over the head or spurs it in the shoulder, or in any other manner abuses or neglects to care for it while in his charge, shall be dismissed from the Company's service."

Mrs. Duke says that she personally never knew a man to be fired from the XIT except for violation of Rule No. 9. "Colonel Boyce often gave a man a second chance if he did not get along with a foreman on one division; he would put him on another division, but he never gave a man a second chance over mistreating a horse. He had to get off the ranch at once, and many a time he had to walk off."

In September, 1906, Mrs. Duke was teaching a four-pupil school in a ranch house on a Texas strip between Oklahoma and the XIT. By this time she had met Bob Duke and they were beginning to be "interested." After returning with her pupils from a late roundup near El Frio Springs on the Cold Water Draw, she was warned by one overgrown boy at dinner, "I tell yuh, Miss Cordia, yuh better not fool with that Bob Duke."

When she looked at him questioningly, the youth elaborated: "I tell yuh, I saw him fire a fellow last Saturday after dinner and he made that cowboy walk twelve miles to Buffalo Springs. The fellow was beating his horse over the head with a stake pin."

Cordia Sloan decided to take her chances anyway.

The next year she saw Bob Duke in action. F. M. Moore, the wagon boss, had sent a man to pick up his check. While the man was in the bunkhouse, Duke walked out toward the barn, where his wife wanted to check some setting hens. Suddenly he stopped, looking down a slope toward the garden, where a horse was standing motionless, head down.

" 'That man rode him almost to death in this heat,' said Bob.

"It was about three o'clock. Bob turned back and went to the bunkhouse. Bob was as weak looking [from meningitis] as the horse was. He went up on the porch and called the man out.

" 'You get going to Channing and you walk. No horse will take you there. Look at that horse! You have rode him almost to death. Now get going!'

"The man did not say a word but got his hat and started on his fifteen-mile walk to Channing. We went in the house; I watched the man across the valley and up the opposite caprock almost three miles away. It was hot. I know that man consigned the XIT and all foremen to perdition that did not consider the rights of a man to treating dumb animals as he wanted to treat them.

"Bob called the office in Channing and told them what he had done. H. S. Boice was in the office, and he surely commended him for it."

One boy was even hired with no other qualification than that he loved horses. Bessie Boyce was the Colonel's favorite, as well as his secretary. At a time when the XIT was fully staffed, a letter came from a farm boy in Maryland, saying he loved cows and horses and wanted to get where he could work with them exclusively. Without getting clearance, Bessie told the farm boy to come on. The Colonel stormed, but gave in to his daughter, since it was too late anyway.

The boy came on, and was an immediate sensation. The first night in the bunkhouse, as the hands prepared for bed, he knelt by his bed and prayed. Said one cowboy the next morning, "It was the first time I had ever seen a cowboy pray, but we all respected his religion." The boy stayed and became a "prime favorite," because he would work at anything and particularly because he loved his horses and cows. And he never stopped his bedside praying.

Mrs. Duke sums up the relationship between horse and man:

"Some cowboys have told me that after they have learned a horse well enough, they know what to expect of him at all times and places. They were amazed when it dawned on them that the horse knew what to expect of them at all times and places. They couldn't fool a horse."

MONTANA

FOR SOME YEARS John V. Farwell experimented
with test-feeding his Texas cattle on more northerly ranges
from Kansas to the Black Hills before he decided in 1890 to
buy a small ranch fifty-nine miles north of Miles City, Montana. Shortly he leased two million acres between the Yellowstone and Missouri rivers, giving XIT ownership five million
acres to oversee. Word went down to the Texas Panhandle
for A. G. Boyce to start ten thousand head toward the Montana spread. Before the Montana summer range closed down,
many an XIT cowboy had learned the route north from Buffalo Springs, the XIT collection spot in Texas. Some became
Montanans for life; to others it was always a foreign land,

curious and likable but no place to live. But those who rode
the sixteen hundred miles up the trail—across Colorado, Wyoming, and half of Montana—never forgot it, and their
reminiscences are studded with tales of life beyond the Yellowstone.

There were all sorts of ways to get there. Arch Sneed took
this route:

"I left Middle Water with forty cars of steers, and there
were three other men with me: two shippers [including
Sneed] and two helpers—John W. Baughman, now of Lib-
eral, Kansas, of Griffin and Baughman, real estate firm of
Liberal; and Oscar Reed, who had been the foreman for
Wadkins of Moore County; and Dick Howden of Bovina,
Texas, afterwards known in Montana as 'Whiskey Dick.'
We unloaded and fed at Lincoln, Nebraska, and rested the
cattle. We had shipped over the Rock Island to Lincoln and
went on the Chicago and Northwestern Railroad from Coun-
cil Bluffs, Iowa, to Oakes, South Dakota. Then we went the
Northern Pacific to Montana. We unloaded and fed again
at Jamestown, North Dakota, and from there we went into
Glendive, where the cattle were unloaded on the south bank
of the Yellowstone River and crossed on a toll bridge, where
they were turned loose on this XIT range.

"Young Albert Boyce was running a roundup wagon and
received the cattle at Glendive, and Cato was the general
manager. Dick Howden went to work for Albert Boyce there.
He asked me if I had come to go to work, and I told him no,
that I was going back to Buffalo Springs. Just after we were
through unloading our train Otho Mims and a young Powell
from Channing, Texas, arrived with a trainload of cattle for
the XIT's. I waited until they were unloaded and we came
back to Texas together."

His greeting was what impressed Emmett Glidewell most
about Montana. A youth who had spent all his life on a farm

about fifteen miles east of Graham, Texas, which was fairly settled country, he was sent by train to Montana. He saw his first XIT hands when the train stopped at Terry, Montana, where six or seven boys who had been to a dance the night before boarded his car. When the men got off at Fallon, they began a five-mile walk to meet the foreman, Bob Fudge, ferrying across the Yellowstone River on their way. It was a beautiful morning.

"About half way to the ranch we met Bob Fudge and the wagon. There on the wagon seat sat 245 pounds dressed in a fur coat and cap driving a big bay and a white horse (known to me later as Chunky and Eagle).

"He was pleased to see the Long boys coming back, and he began to cuss them, calling them names. I felt like crawling under the wagon for fear he'd start on me next, as I had never heard greetings like that. We went on to the ranch, and on the walls hung fur coats, fur caps, and fur chaps. Montana seemed to me more wonderful than I had ever pictured it to be.

"We were all put on the payroll the first day of April, 1905. We were all Texas boys. Cato, the general manager, was from Texas, too. Our first work was to patch the mess tent and the bed tent. It took several days to gather the cow ponies for the spring roundup. At last the wagon pulled out. None more happy and excited than I."

One year A. G. Boyce decided it would be easier to trail his steers to Montana if he sent along a herd of heifers to help locate the steers and keep them from drifting too much. All the two-year-old off-colored heifers were gathered and fed into the herd of steers as they set off for the long walk to Montana.

"If I ever knew," writes J. W. Standifer, who went along, "whether it served the purpose or not, I have forgotten now. At the time it only meant a lot of extra work for us."

A. L. Denby's memory is much clearer. According to him, he went north to Montana with the first herd of XIT cattle in the spring of 1890. The herd was split into three parts, with John Carlos trailing the lead herd, Ab Owings the second, and Bill Coats the third. Coats was boss for Denby.

"We loaded out of Channing the tenth of May and shipped to Windower [Wendover], Wyoming. We started out from there with instructions to drift north into Montana until stopped by George Findlay and O. C. Cato, who had driven ahead in a buckboard to find a location. George Findlay, manager of the Chicago office, supervised the starting of the herds and received them when they arrived in Montana.

"The herd was stopped on the head of Cedar Creek, Custer County, Montana, the first of August and turned loose there. We were all furnished with a horse apiece and a chuck wagon as far as Windower, Wyoming. From there we were given a pass back to Channing.

"Some of the men who were in this first trail herd were John Flowers, Tom McHenry, Dick Maybree, Steve Beebe, Frank Freeland, and the boss Bill Coats. These were all Texas men. Also a colored man by name of Charlie who lived at Tascosa and Channing. He was the horse wrangler. When we got to Wyoming, Billy Wilson and another one named Tony joined the outfit. When the boss asked Tony what his name was he said that over at the VT where he had been working they called him a little son of a ————. The boss told him that if it made no particular difference to him they wouldn't call him that.

"Of this bunch my pal John Flowers and I are the only ones living (February 14, 1937) that I know of. He lives about sixty miles above Miles City on the Tongue River.

"The winter after the first drive John Flowers worked on Bravo and I wintered in Wichita Falls. The spring of 1891 I went back to Channing. The year before there had been little more than stock pens and a section house. This spring of ninety-one there was a fine hotel and quite a town had sprung up. XIT headquarters had been moved there. You may find it hard to believe but there was also a saloon run by Jim and Bob East. I heard later there was no saloon there because the XIT would not stand for it.

"That spring there were four herds driven to Montana. John Flowers and I came back with Bill Coats as boss again. We left from Buffalo Springs early in May, 1891. As well as I can remember, Milt Whipple drove the first herd. Ealy Moore and Ab Owings each drove one, and Bill Coats the tail herd.

"We started across the strip thirty miles wide and then known as No Man's Land. It is now a part of Oklahoma. We had got one day's drive into the strip when word came back to us to turn-tail herd back to Buffalo Springs as quick as we could. Government inspectors had arrested Owings and Whipple and were holding up their herds. We were crossing the strip without a permit. Our herd got back over the line to Buffalo Springs and had to wait until Boyce and Findlay got our permit and paid for the other herds."

Starting again, with "green broncs but one gentle night horse," the herd made it into Colorado, where a blizzard hit.* Before it subsided half the horses had been lost, though all the herd was saved. Farther along, on the Belle Fourche, Denby quit, "but the herd landed in Montana with as many head as they started with because they kept catching a few head lost by the lead herds." Denby meanwhile had drifted over to Deadwood for a month and on to Buffalo, Wyoming. Autumn found him working for the U cross spread, about twenty miles from Buffalo.

* See Chapter on "Weather," pp. 161–162.

"I was there when the Johnson County war started between the cattlemen and the rustlers. The cattlemen hired gunmen from Texas and started out to kill off the rustlers. They succeeded in killing several and burning their ranches. The rustlers finally got organized and rounded up the cattlemen at the old TA ranch on Powder River. The rustlers had them surrounded and were tunneling in to them by breastworks built on wagon wheels, and very nearly reached them. In the meantime one of the cattlemen had escaped and gone to Fort McKinney for soldiers. The soldiers got there just in the nick of time to save the cattlemen from being massacred. The soldiers arrested the cattlemen and tried them for murder of the rustlers but nothing was ever done about it. Most of the rustlers left Wyoming and drifted up into Montana and Canada.

"That winter and next summer I came to Montana and worked for the JO ranch on Tongue River. My pal John Flowers also worked there that winter.

"In the spring of 1893 we both went back to work for the XIT and worked there continuously until they closed out in 1898.

"O. C. Cato was then manager of the Cedar Creek Ranch, the only XIT ranch in Montana at the time. He run two wagons; Sam Akre was foreman of one and Henry Ross foreman of the other.

"In 1895 the XIT bought the Hatchett Ranch, six miles from Fallon, Montana, and made it headquarters. In 1898 the XIT closed out and O. C. Cato, the manager, and S. Johnson bought out the ranch and the she stuff; their brand was the Star Bar C. In 1902 Cato and Johnson took thirty thousand XIT cattle to run. At the end of that year the company decided they could run them cheaper themselves; so they gave Cato ten thousand for his contract and put him back in as manager of the XIT. This was in the spring of 1903. Cato had been elected sheriff of Custer County, Montana, in 1898 and served until spring of 1903.

"I went back to work for the XIT at the same time and stayed until they closed out again in 1909. I worked as ranchman and skiffman, swimming herds across the Yellowstone in the fall.

"Mr. Cato died in 1915. He was state senator from Custer County at the time. He was one of the best men I ever knew and one of the best cowmen. He would very near tell the color of a cow by looking at her track.

"The old Hatchett Ranch and land was sold to the government by the Cato heirs. About twenty-five years ago this country was settled up and the people tried to make a farming country of it. They nearly all starved out and now most of them are working for the government. The government has bought a lot of land in here and is reseeding it to grass and planning on making a grazing section of it again. L. D. McMakin and I still live on the old range, he about a mile from the old ranch, which has been all torn down, and I about three miles.

"I mentioned my being skiffman. In those days the Yellowstone was some river, big, and very swift. If we got off to a good start the cattle were taken in swimming water by the cowpunchers, and two skiffmen could then handle them. Maybe have them across in thirty minutes. If they didn't get started before sunup, or if there was a wind, it was sometimes pretty hard to get started. We would strip to our underclothes and take saddles from the horses and go in bareback. If a man had a green horse that had never worked in the river he was apt to go to lunging and sinking instead of swimming. Then the skiffs would have to rescue the man. Often when we got a bad start cowboys and horses had to swim to get across with the cattle. Late in October we would have to cross in a snowstorm."

The man who wrote the most detailed account of XIT life in Montana is J. K. Marsh, who left behind what amounts to a guide to ranch practices.

"The work on the open range plan in Montana was very different from the work in Texas, where all land was owned or controlled and fenced. The eastern division of the general roundup started at the mouth of Custer Creek on the Yellowstone, between the twentieth and the twenty-fifth of May each year.

"In 1905 there was the XIT wagon with Rufe Morris [as] wagon boss and captain of the roundup. As it was on XIT range, he planned all of the work, such as saying where they would round up, and the XIT got all of the mavericks.

"With the CK wagon with Dave Claire as wagon boss and the Buttleman Pool wagon with Ernest Long as wagon boss, we worked down the Yellowstone to Deer Creek and met the Charley Creek (Pot Hound) Pool, H. A. Miller, wagon boss, and the Bar Diamond, Frank Weinrich, wagon boss. Then we all worked together to Burns Creek and up the North Fork of Burns Creek to Fox Lake. Then over the divide onto East Red Water, where Dave Claire took charge of the roundup.

"The Lazy J wagon, Hugh Exum, wagon boss, met us on East Red Water, and we worked down East Red Water and up Red Water to the old Circle Ranch, where we met the LU wagon, Lawrence Higgins, wagon boss; then the Pool and Bar Diamond wagons turned back.

"The rest of us worked on up Red Water to the head, and down Timber Creek to the Big Dry, then across to the Woody, and down the Big Dry to the Missouri River. Then down it to Sand Creek, and up the Divide to Nelson Lake, and the finish—and the outfits all scattered.

MONTANA

Missouri River

Musselshell R.

Yellowstone River

MILES CITY
FORT KEOGH
XIT

GLENDIVE
FALLON
TERRY

WYOMING

Powder River

North Platte R.

Belle Fourche R.

DEADWOOD

LUSK

WENDOVER

NEBRASKA

COLORADO

South Platte R.

Platte River

BRUSH

BOVINA

Big Sandy Creek

KIT CARSON
CHIVINGTON

LAMAR

Arkansas River

KANSAS

DODGE CITY

Arkansas River

TRINIDAD

SPRINGFIELD

SPRINGER

BUFFALO SPRINGS

CHANNING

TASCOSA

Cimarron R.

North Canadian R.

Canadian River

OKLAHOMA

Red River

YELLOW HOUSES

COLORADO CITY

TEXAS

Inset map

Milk R.

CK

N—

Poplar R.

Missouri River

Big Dry Cr.

Little Dry Cr.

XIT

BOW AND ARROW

Yellowstone River

Musselshell R.

Redwater Cr.

O'Fallon Cr.

Cedar Cr.

Timber Cr.

Cherry Cr.

GLENDIVE
FALLON
TERRY

LUBAR

FORT KEOGH
MILES CITY

Powder River

Little Powder R.

Pumpkin Cr.

Mizpah Cr.

Powder River

EASTERN MONTANA

SCALE OF MILES
0   25   50

Legend

XIT TRAILS

•••••••• Montana Trail
············ Yellow Houses-Colorado City
|||||||||||| Tascosa - Dodge City
– – – – Tascosa - Springer
xxxxxxxxxxxx Buffalo Springs-Trinidad

SCALE OF MILES
0   65   130

"I was working for the CK outfit at that time and I forgot to state that we met with the Hat X (Hugh Wells was range manager and Glenn Hollingsworth was wagon boss) on Hungry Creek, and they worked with us to the finish.

"With five wagons working together, there were around 125 men on circle every morning, and sometimes as many as 200 at the roundup, as there were a lot of what we called 'dinner reps' (small stockmen who lived in the vicinity and came to the roundup to get their cattle, and usually borrowed a horse from some outfit, and stayed for dinner and supper, and got theirs branded, and talked some cook out of a chunk of beef to take home).

"When working down the Yellowstone and up Red Water the XIT killed a yearling at least every day, and sometimes every night, for a week at a time.

"Red Water drains a country about a hundred miles long and from forty to sixty miles wide, and with the big crews we circled both sides at the same time on the general round-up. I have seen day after day, working up Red Water, where there would be an estimated fifteen thousand cattle on the roundup ground and where there were five wagons working together, the roundup would be cut into five bunches. Each outfit would take a bunch and work, and they would follow each other from one roundup to another until everybody was through. They would cut out the cows and calves first into a common bunch, and a couple of cowboys would be sent to hold them on water until after supper at five o'clock. After supper, we branded, as we rarely got the roundup all thrown together until two o'clock, and usually finished up working it around four or a little later.

"Any stockman running five hundred head and up had representatives commonly called 'reps' and the XIT and CK only carried a rep herd on Red Water, but the other outfits carried everything and would throw back to the home

range every few days. The 79, LU, Cross K, Hat X, and Bow
and Arrow, and Lazy J had reps with the XIT or CK wagons
until we met the western wagons; then they cut out and went
to those wagons and carried their cattle in those herds.

"It was quite a sight to see five outfits camped along the
creek with the five remudas and herds scattered along for
four-five miles on the creek. It was sometimes hard for a new
man to find his own outfit. I recall one time when a fellow
had just gone to work for one of the wagons. He went out
and dayherded all afternoon for the wrong outfit. Of course,
an old head was to blame for it and had a lot of fun
over it.

"We had breakfast between three and four in the morning,
dinner at eleven and supper at five. We had to stand two
hours' guard at night, about every third night when we had
a big crew, and oftener if the crew got cut down for any
reason. On the beef work in the fall it was guard every
night when we had a herd, which we always did, except
when going back to gather another one. As it got later in the
fall we stood five guards, two men to the guard. First and
last guards were three hours; sometimes last guard was longer, as you stayed out there until you were relieved after
breakfast.

"The XIT always made five shipments of two trains each,
with each wagon every fall; and once or twice we shipped
three trains with Morris's wagon. The wagons shipped on al-
ternate weeks, which made each wagon ship every two weeks
and finished up around the first of November. Then they un-
shod the horses and laid off all the men but six, counting the
two wagon bosses. Rufe Morris kept his cook and L. D. Mc-
Makin and Bob Fudge kept his cook and the Hatchett ranchman, Al Denby.

"Rufe and his outfit stayed at the XIT Ranch and Bob
stayed at the Hatchett. The horses were all turned loose on

Cedar Creek, near the XIT. Any man that was going to work for the outfit the following year could pick his string for a horse to ride through the winter. If they refused to let a man keep up a horse he might just as well figure he was going to work for some other outfit next year.

"There was no winter work in the country at that time to amount to anything, and the boys used to make the two ranches their headquarters and took in all the dances in the country during the winter. Girls were very scarce and any cowboy who managed to spear himself a steady girl was considered a little above the rest, or he usually felt that way anyhow. But the saying was that no cowboy could summer a girl or winter a slicker, although in some instances it was done. It was very seldom that a school marm taught the second term without annexing some cowboy for a husband, and as a rule they had the entire bunch to pick from.

"I went to Montana in 1904 and went to work for the CK outfit at Glendive in June, as they were working down the river on the general roundup, and worked that fall until the wagon pulled off the last of November. I worked for them through the general in 1905 and quit in August and went to work for Rufe Morris on Red Water, when he was gathering his second beef herd, and worked until the wagon pulled off the first of November. In 1906 we started to work at the mouth of Custer Creek on the twentieth day of May. Both XIT wagons were there, as the western roundups did not start until later than usual, and Bob Fudge had to start receiving cattle at Glendive around June 12 from the Southern XIT Ranch.

"On account of so many western cattle being handled in our territory in 1905 the XIT and CK refused to handle them with reps. So it was arranged at the stock meeting in Miles City, when they laid out the roundups for the year, that the Hat X wagon come down, Charles Bell wagon boss. We worked Custer Creek and made one roundup on Cherry Creek, and it started raining. We never turned a wheel for eight days, tried to roundup a time or two but had to quit. We lost twelve days on account of rain between Custer Creek and Glendive, and twenty-two days altogether on general, and never finished up until the middle of August.

"That was the rainiest year I ever saw in Montana, except 1915.

"We pulled off the wagon, I think, on the second day of November, and the outfit had a lot of railroad land leased around the XIT Ranch but did not have furrows plowed around it, which was the law against sheep. When we got to the ranch we found John Howe with three bands of sheep grazing right up to the door. So we got a surveyor out there to find corners and Ed Weisner and I put four horses on a walking plow and followed those surveyors around over the hills and coulees for days, plowing furrows and setting up trespass notices until it snowed. Perhaps some people think we liked that job. The winter of 1906–1907 was a stem-winder, and it cost John Howe a lot of money to try to eat the XIT out, as he got caught in there; and after we got the land all marked he did not have much range and could not get out. He lost 90 per cent of his sheep.

"The snow started the last of November and never let up; by Christmas we would not get away from the ranch, except to go after the mail at McMillan post office once a week. Ten miles. It was a long day's work to go there and back. We used to bring the mail for Grue Brothers and Ledson Brothers, who lived a few miles away from the ranch.

"Ed Weisner bought the ferry at Fallon that winter, which left me as next oldest man, and I was kept on the payroll that winter. Rufe Morris sent word to McMakin and I, in February, to come to the Hatchett. We left the XIT before sunup, riding big-grained horses, and got to the Undem Ranch after dark, fifteen miles, and left there next morning at daylight. We got to the Hatchett a little after noon, and that was only ten miles.

"We saw as many as sixteen head of cattle in one bunch dead. Thousands of cattle had drifted on to the Yellowstone, and the snow was four feet deep on the level on the Yellowstone Flat. We cut the Northern Pacific fence and let them drift into the bad lands on the south side of the river. Bob Fudge had to take his wagon over in the spring and gather them; the CK had a wagon over there the next fall. The XIT put in a lot of Texas yearlings in the spring of 1905, but they never shipped out very many of them; the snow was so deep they could not get to it and their legs got so sore from climbing through the deep snow that they would just quit and die.

"Rufe Morris was a very good beef man and always got his herds to the road in good shape. The southern fellows were good hands, but not such good beef hands the first year or two. They did not like dayherding and were too keen with their ropes, which did not 'go' around a beef herd, as one little run would knock $1,000.00 off the herd.

"The sheep is what put the XIT out of business when they did. The settlers never started to come in here until 1909, and only a few then. Some school marms took up some claims on the flats south of Fallon in 1909 and came to the Hatchett dance that winter and thought there were no cowboys there because they did not have their chaps and spurs on.

"Mr. O. C. Cato was general manager there, and a finer man never lived, but was death on whiskey around the outfit when they were working. He was willing for the boys to go to town when they had time and get drunk and get it off of their minds, but there was no drinking around the wagons and no poker playing either.

"Bob Fudge was a big man; he weighed around 250 in

the winter and around 230 in the summer,* but was very light and easy on horses. He was a real cowman but had trouble running a wagon, for when anything went wrong he could not help but say something to the man when they both were mad, and most cowboys were very touchy."

The Texas boys liked to make the trek to Montana. It might be a long and arduous haul, but it represented change. Besides, there were always a few days on the town before starting back. "The town" was Miles City, which Gene Elliston remembers as a "typical western town; every one carried the law on his hip, gambling houses was thick, all wide open, saloons—the whiskey flowed in all directions. The red lights was doing a great business.

"The first thing the cowboys done was to run the soldiers out of town, which was easy, as you know a soldier can't do much without orders. So we cowboys celebrated in a grand way."

To an XIT hand, coming along largely after the open range had been put under fence, Montana played the same role that Abilene, Wichita, and Dodge had filled for an earlier generation of Texas cowboys. It might not be heaven on earth, but it was somewhere to go, an interruption and an interlude in a life that lost its daily monotone only when looking backward and remembering.

* Some hands place the figure around 325 pounds.

WEATHER

FEW PEOPLE in the United States who read periodicals or listen to comedians have been able to escape exposure to jokes about how incredibly cold or incredibly dry or incredibly windy or incredibly sandy the weather is likely to be around Amarillo. Although some of the stories are obviously inventions and are strained and stretched beyond either belief or humor, there is no denying the Texas Panhandle weather indulges in extremes and is often something to wonder at. Nor can it be denied that, for all the notoriety surrounding Amarillo, the weather in Dalhart, Channing, and other points in or along the XIT country is even more extreme. And finally, it should be added that one reason why

Texans perpetrate such outlandish stories about weather on
the plains is that weather is continually on their minds, and
is a more continuously absorbing subject, whether simply for
discussing or for outwitting, than in almost any other portion
of the United States.

XIT cowboys, then, are merely behaving like other prod-
ucts of their Panhandle environment when they write about
weather. It stung their eyes, and got them lost. It held them
on the banks of the Canadian River, on its annual "tare,"
trying to keep four thousand cattle content till they could be
crossed. It was forever a factor in their work, and it was also
perennially unpredictable. Listen, for instance, to how it
affected Bob Field:

"The next morning after the storm I and Chickasaw, another cowboy, rode over to the Matthews and Reynolds camp.
There was three long X horses laying there dead with the
saddles on, staked. The cowboys had not got up and the
cook was still asleep. They were covered in about seven or
eight inches of snow. We hollered at them to come out of the
hay, and they said they did not have any wood to cook anything with and to keep warm by. So we taken the trail the
way their cattle drifted and followed them by dead cattle and
dead horses. That led us to Hugo, Colorado, and there was
where we found all the horses, cattle, and men.

"I was about seventeen years old at this time, and it happened at Dan Cole's wagon that day two men, one named
George, and Berkley Howell, wanted to quit Dan Cole, and
Cole told them that he did not want to hire them in the first
place and now that he was in a tight he would not let them
quit. Then he said, 'I will kill you both before you will quit
me this kind of weather and in a tight.' I believe Mr. Cole
would have killed both these men if they had insisted to quit
him in this kind of a tight. The XIT had a racket over the division of cattle, as each one wanted to count out his number

of cattle up on Cedar Creek, Montana, up where they were
taking these cattle, each claiming that their cattle did not die.
The way I remember it Mr. Cole got the big end of the deal.
Mr. Cole was a kind of a game old rooster."

Field tells a bitter story about an unseasonable snowstorm
that hit a herd he was taking north in company with several
other herds. The year was 1892, the time was June 2, and
the place was a camp about two miles north of Hell Springs,
Colorado. Field had 3100 two-year-olds under his care.

"Dan Cole was driving an XIT herd and they were camped
about ten miles southwest of Hell Springs. Chris Gish, with
an XIT herd, was camped about six miles south of Hell
Springs. Matthews and Reynolds was camped southeast of us
about five miles. They were driving a long X herd. All these
herds contained about three thousand cattle each. There were
some more herds which I cannot remember who was trailing
them through. It commenced raining and snowing about four
in the evening. The herds all got away and got together at
Hugo, Colorado, about twenty-five miles off. And the cowpunchers all got together there in the saloon.

"So the next day we put in the biggest part of the day looking up some boys who did not make it back to the wagons,
which we found to have frozen down. Flannel-eyed Frank
and Bob Blackwell rode their two horses until they froze
down on them and died. They used their horses for wind-
breaks to keep from freezing to death. Frank was frozen until
he was unconscious; Blackwell was so cold he was helpless.
We found these men about ten o'clock the next day; we
packed Frank on a horse like you would a dead man. We carried them into camp. When they began to thaw out I have
never seen anyone suffer such misery. It scared us all so bad
we did not know what to do. So we took him to a German's
house over next the railroad and they helped take care of

him, as they had had some experience in taking care of frozen men. We left him a horse there and in about ten days he come on the outfit.

"All the cowboys got together there at Hugo, Colorado, and the cattle were all together. We elected Dan Cole as general manager to work these cattle. This was some steer herd, all together. We cut them into six herds to work them. I think, if I remember right, we had 86 cattle to freeze to death out of our herd. Out of the total of the herds there were somewhere close to about 500 cattle froze to death in this spell. Matthews and Reynolds lost about 400 head. XIT lost about 20 head of horses, and Matthew and Reynolds lost about 25 head of horses out of 75."

Gene Elliston, who wrote at length, and vividly, about all facets of XIT life, tells this weather story:

"I noticed around the northern horizon clouds began to form. We began putting the herd over the fence into Rito Blanco Pasture about five o'clock in the evening. It was snowing so hard we could hardly see what we were doing. If the storm had hit us an hour sooner we would have lost the herd; we could not have helt them in that blinding snow.

"As soon as we got them across the fence we throwed them into the Alamositas Canyon, which was nearby and easy done. The cattle was like the cowboys—looking for shelter. It was the first canyon they had ever seen; so it did not take long to settle them down, the weather having something to do with it. We turned and headed south for the ranch house and where our chuck wagon was. When we got there the cook had another one of those steaming hot suppers—beefsteak, coffee, and prunes and a big rolling hot fire. The fireplace was about five feet wide and five feet high. It was chucked full of cottonwood logs and the flames was rolling high. Oh say, boy, what a life! One got good and warm and filled up on that supper, made down our hot rolls, and you know what happened. But before we went to bed here's what we did.

"The ranch house had a window in the north side close to the fireplace and one in the south side opposite. Our wood was all big cottonwood logs, and our ax looked like the teeth in a crosscut saw, that is the edge of it did. So we slipped the windows back a little and went out to the wood pile, taken four men to the log, and histed it through the south window, jammed the ends of those logs into that fireplace, and as the cook had not lost as much sleep as the rest of us, he had an alarm clock he would wake up and look the fire over. When the ends burned off he called for help and some of us would get up and move our logs in. So we fared fine.

"Morning came too quick, but when it came it was still blowing and snowing. So we stayed there all day, slept and ate, not much talking. It quit snowing about noon, so the next morning we started, found our cattle scattered from Alamositas fence to the Canadian River, pretty well all in the canyon. We came on that day to the Punta de Agua River and camped on the north side of it, stood guard that night, and the next day the boss told me to catch me a pack horse to go to the ranch, as they would turn the cattle loose that day. And I came in the next day.

"Oh, boy, I felt good. I soon had my bed packed on a horse that I led, and rode one crossing the river. I did, so on the ice it did not break through. Now you have the problem solved why hair grows on a man's breast—when he stays on, something has got to grow there.* Was not a man on the job who washed on this trip, unless it was the cook, and I am not sure about him. I will state right here that that was one snow I appreciated. It fell at the right time. But I

* If this is incomprehensible to the reader so is it to the editor.

imagine now sometimes I can still hear those cattle bawling."

When W. A. Askew was a toddler, he lived near Marble Falls, in the central part of Texas. Often he would listen and wonder at the blasts going off four miles from his home, not realizing, of course, that in a sense these blasts would determine his livelihood a decade in the future and several hundred miles in the distance. For the blasts were issuing from a nearby quarry, from which stone was being shipped to help build the new state capitol at Austin. Any payment for the stone and other expenses entailed in construction would ultimately come from the XIT, not then established. And so young Askew went to school three or four months a year until he was sixteen, when his family pooled its resources to buy him a rail ticket to Goodnight, Texas, away to the north and west.

When Askew arrived, in early January, he was wearing a thin suit of clothes, "Seersucker, by name." Outside a blizzard was howling. From that time forward it must have seemed to him that blizzards dogged his steps throughout the Panhandle. At first he worked for Colonel Charles Goodnight, considered by many to be the finest cowman who ever lived. But after a year the Colonel sold out, and Askew was "out of a job in the dead of winter."

"I saddled my private horse, shipped my bed to Channing, straddled my horse, and started out. I stayed all night in Amarillo and lingered there next morning until about 10 A.M. and then started to Channing. I went about twenty miles, and it began to snow, and all traces of a trail was covered up, but I kept going in the direction I thought I should go.

"I had traveled all day, and when night came I looked in every direction. The snow was at least ten inches deep, and I saw a faint light south of me and I turned towards it. I was at least ten miles north of where I should have gone. I arrived in Channing about 9:30 P.M. and took my horse to the livery stable and fed him and rubbed him off, because he had traveled about seventy-five miles that day without food or water. I went to the hotel and there was no room for me; therefore I just sat in a chair until about 1 A.M. and a Mexican came in and said he had a bed over at his house, and I went over, and I paid him before I went to bed, because I told him that I wanted to get out early, and he put me in a nice room, clean sheets and all, for twenty-five cents. I thought I was dreaming.

"Next morning early I went to see about my horse, and he seemed to be all right after a hard day's ride; I ate breakfast at a restaurant and went out on the street, and a freighter drove up to a store and I went over to see him, and see if I could find anything pertaining to a job; he said he was freighting for the XIT from the Rito Blanco Division, and he did not know if a cowhand was needed or not, but he said if I would go with him, I could hang around for a week as a regular sweater and nothing would be charged against me.

"We traveled almost all day and went as fast as we could behind four good mules; there were no roads that we could see, as we had eight or ten inches of snow on the ground. We arrived at the ranch headquarters, and it was almost dark. The boss came out and the cowhand talked to him for a short time and asked him, 'Who is the fellow with you?' and he told him I was a cowhand looking for work. The boss asked me several questions and then said, 'Turn your horse loose in the horse pasture and throw your bedroll in the doghouse.'

"We did little jobs around there for a few days and the chuck wagon was prepared for a trip, I knew not where. We were told to hitch certain horses to the wagon, and a cowhand and myself were to drive to the Canadian River, find a camping place, and build a corral for five horses. We reached the river about nightfall and no good camping place was to be found there; so we crossed the river. We came near losing our wagon in the quicksand, but we got over. The snow was still deep.

"When we found a small spring running down a small ravine where there was plenty of cottonwood trees growing, there we camped. We hobbled our horses and fixed our beds and ate some supper out of cans. We put our beds in the wagon. Next morning we could not see a horse; but we got them—they were trying to go back to the ranch, but didn't get very far on account of the hobbles."

One Panhandle storm caught Frank Shardelman with more than the usual responsibilities; he also had seventy-two–year–old Uncle Jack Leonard. They were moving "the Matlock dipping vat from up near Buffalo Springs to Rito Blanco and was caught in one of the worst blizzards to sweep the Panhandle country. From Middle Water to the cap rocks west of Rito Blanco we followed the old buffalo trails that were beat deep in paths; I walked all the way to keep the team from getting into them and overturning our wagons. The only way I could tell where they were was when I would step into them. But I brought Uncle Jack in safe, bundled up in his bed blankets."

In the spring of 1891 an XIT herd hit the trail north from Buffalo Springs for Montana, only to be turned back when it crossed the narrow strip now comprising Oklahoma's Panhandle. Starting again with green mounts, the cowpunchers trailed the herd into Colorado, when a blizzard struck. Askew describes the situation.

"We were all about afoot then with these worn-out broncs. Then when the blizzard struck we couldn't get them out of a walk and couldn't hold the cattle. The cattle paid no attention to six-shooters or slickers. Just walked around our horses and on again. So we lost all the horses but a few head and the wagon horses. The boss gave orders to hitch to the wagon, turn the cattle loose, and follow them. About dark they drifted into some cedar breaks on the head of a creek. We camped the wagon on the edge of the breaks.

"About dark the storm stopped. It cleared up and the moon came out. The boss had us ride through the breaks and out on the other side and circle to see if any stock came out of the breaks. We found that they hadn't; so we went back and built big cedar fires, staked our horses, scattered around in the breaks two together, and slept on our saddle blankets in the snow. Next morning at daylight we started out to round 'em up. By eleven o'clock we had the herd rounded up and counted. We hadn't lost a hoof. But we had lost about half the horses, which we never did find. We had to buy new horses to come on up the trail. We had no more trouble after that except a night run once in a while."

Cattle, not noted for their intelligence, seemed to possess intuitive judgment when faced with bad weather. Ina Chillcut recalls one blizzard in which the camp where she was living was snowed in for three days. Everyone wondered about the cattle, but they came through.

"In storms like this the dumb brutes had no protection but a draw or ravine. The horses would run but the cows would hump their backs to the storms, and in draws the heat would melt snow so that it would form ice and make a covering over them. The coyotes would howl; it took faith to match the loneliness and awful weather. But when the dawn appeared, what is more glorious—a red glow over the blue sky, and such a white world, and how far the least sound carries in the still air. The stock take on new life, begin running about, and the snowbirds are in flocks."

A complaint against the dryness comes from Mrs. Allen Willbanks, who writes as follows:

"Water was so scarce at that time that we could scarcely

keep water to drill with. We got without water one time in August, and we started our man out to find water. He went from one well to the other, and the wells, or tanks, were all dry, due to the fact that there was not enough wind to turn the mills to pump the water. Sox, our man, had to keep on going until he found water. He was gone two days and one night before he found water. Once he had to go over into Oklahoma to get the water. We got entirely out of water for our babies. Stella and Ovida were the babies then. So about two o'clock the last day we saw a covered wagon crossing the country about a mile way. Mr. Willbanks went up on the hill close to camp and called these people until they answered and stopped. He went over to them and asked if they had any drinking water for our babies, and they gave us all they had, and this was just a cupful or two they had left from the dregs from dinner. This lasted until late in the evening, when we heard our man coming over the hills hallooing. Mr. Willbanks would answer back to his calls until he came in sight to let us know he was near with water.

"The whole country was dry enough most of the time that we could strike a match and drop it and set the whole country on fire, excepting the first spring we came to this country; we had so much rain we could hardly drive across the prairies without bogging down. This was about the tenth of May, 1900.

"We had plenty of snow and rain at intervals, the same as we do now. We moved from Mr. Tobe Pitts' division to Mr. Jo Cluck's division. This was in the fall of 1904. This was a dreadful winter—our feet froze from the cold weather. We suffered due to the fact that we did not have anything to burn for fuel but cow chips and the scrap lumber from the windwill towers we erected, of which I helped my husband saw the lumber to build the towers, helped him run the drill and run the horse power, later helped run the gasoline engine. Helped him put the casing in the wells and did a man's work (I have wandered away from my subject).

"They had a colored man on the ranch that they called Jim. He was a good Negro man. Everybody thought lots of old Jim. He would come to our camp and spend the night when he had to bring out a load of casing or rods for the windmills. One time when he came out he made out his hot roll, or bed, in a teepee we had for the men to sleep in, and away in the night one of the coldest snowstorms came up. Mr. Willbanks called Jim and told him to bring his bed into the shack we were living in or he would freeze to death. He did come in and made his bed down on the floor.

"The next morning Jim built the fire, and he said, 'I tell you, Mr. Willbanks, you would have had a dead shine in camp if you had not called me into the house last night.' After that Jim would slip off to our camp and bring us eggs, chickens, or anything else he could get to bring us to eat. He thought so much of us that Mr. Willbanks would tease me and say that I would give him, Jim, the best chair in the front room to smoke his Meerschaum pipe to make me mad.

"Every day was spent pretty much alike. In the spring of the year we had heavy March winds just the same as we do now. The only difference, we found the country was in grass and the dust did not bother us so badly. We have had terrible hail and electric storms, have experienced cold weather that froze the cattle to death and they were banked up by the fence of the Fort Worth and Denver Railway against the fence for miles, a terrible loss to the XIT people."

Not too much is said about sand and dust, probably for two reasons. Blowing sand, while uncomfortable, did not hamper ranching operations as winter blasts did. But more than that, the country round about had not been put to the plow, and essentially wouldn't be for another generation, so that the grass cover and top soil were undisturbed, and considering the wind, dust storms were at a minimum. The High Plains was a paradise of grass—only, man! it could turn miserable in a moment and leave you without a landmark in any direction!

SOUR DOUGH AND SUPPLIES

LIKE SOME OVERSIZED STEER the old chuck wagon trailed along with the cows and cowboys to become an imperishable part of any Western ranching scene. Laden with all sorts of cowpunchers' needs, from bedrolls and prunes to beans and bacon, the wagon was the mobile home, dining room, and kitchen for all hands. Standing fiercely by was the crabbed individualist who would sooner poison a finicky hand than look at him. Wearing a flour-sack apron, he tended the coffee mill, fed his fire from the chip wagon, superintended the Dutch oven with its sour-dough biscuits rising, and loaded the old potrack with its pots, skillets, and coffeepot. When the chuck was ready, he rang a bell, or beat a triangle or skillet.

Bob Duke liked to say that running a ranch successfully required " a prompt pay check and three square meals a day; they will do anything for you." Fred Graven agreed with him: "I sometimes think that cooking has made most of the trouble in the world," he writes. When Duke would assign boys for winter camp, about December 1, he would let them choose their partners, believing that by spring they would be so weary of each other's cooking they would need every bit of pre-friendship possible.

In summer the fare wasn't so monotonous. Since each headquarters had plenty of water to irrigate, each also had a large garden with a good supply of green vegetables. A somewhat different version of ranch diet is given by Frank Shardelman.

"Beef was the main dish, with sour-dough biscuits, rice, beans, and dried fruit—and plenty of good black coffee at all times. Seldom did we get potatoes 'too bulky' to haul, and when they sing about bacon sizzling in the pan do not connect that with a big cattle company's roundup wagon. Beef was sliced and cooked in large pots—called Dutch ovens— partly filled with tallow. And what was called a potrack? Two iron stakes drove in the ground and a rod across the top. The pots were hung from the bar with pothooks and over a trench where the fire was built. What couldn't be fried was usually left for the coyotes to gnaw on. Sometimes the boys would roast the marrow bones over the coals and eat the marrow. Northern wagons would cook beef stew in cold or rainy weather; but the southern states' roundup wagons had a dish for such occasions that no one but a dyed-in-the-wool South Texan or Mexican could eat at first attempt. It was called S.O.B.

"It was made from a short yearling, taking the small intestines, or marrow gut, heart, liver, chop them up in small pieces, add tallow and small bits of beef. Cook as stew, add salt to taste. Then add chili powder until it was almost hot enough to blaze. Then it was ready to serve. The boys that were used to it would fill their plates, grab a sour-dough biscuit and a tin of coffee. The meal was on. But for me, I almost burned down the first time I tried it, but learned to tone it down with rice or beans until I got seasoned to it."

Usually a calf would be killed every other day. If any nester had a dugout nearby, the XIT would send over a beef quarter, which undoubtedly made his week happier. The gift, in part, was generosity, and, in part, hard-headed practicality. Some of the beef would likely spoil before all of it could be eaten, and besides, the XIT hands were instructed always to remember that their employers wished to sell land in time to these farmers. Besides, Bob Duke would always charge his cooks to "cook extra" and to "build" a cake whenever the wagons approached a town, especially Channing, for "the people there could smell fresh beef for several miles."

Once, so the story goes, when Colonel Boyce was manager, the wagon camped over at Two Mile, so called because it was two miles west of Channing. Boyce's daughter, Bessie, decided to ride out to supper at the wagon. The whole town of Channing followed behind. When she saw them filing in, she went to the cook and said: "I am going home. You couldn't have prepared enough for this crowd." He hadn't.

So home went Bessie Boyce. And the whole town followed, unfulfilled and unfilled.

Not so lucky as the foregoing camp cook was Mrs. Allen Willbanks, who hadn't gone West to cook but merely to be a good wife and mother.

"One morning while we were drilling in the Matlock Pasture we were out of groceries; we thought Mr. Willbanks was fixing to send the boy that was helping us into Head Camp for groceries. We looked up and saw a little stream of smoke go high up into the air. This looked like a whirlwind. Mr. Willbanks said, 'Wait a minute, Earnest; take out your team and plough fireguards around the camp or we will be burned out.' Before he could unhitch our mules from the wagon the fire was plainly to be seen and all the cowboys were following the fire-fighting. These men fought fire until late into the night, about nine o'clock.

"Mr. Tobe Pitts came riding up and called me and asked me if I could cook supper for seventy-five men. I told him I would feed them as long as there was a bite left. Me and my husband fed these men, and along towards midnight Mr. Pitts called me and asked me if I could feed forty hungry men, and I told him I would. We fed these men and along towards day he called me again to feed forty for breakfast. We fed them on what we had in camp: meat, sour-dough bread, potatoes, and syrup."

When the cook came in off the range in late autumn, he usually turned to freighting—to Texline, Dalhart, Channing, or Tascosa. He hauled anything—salt, coal, groceries, brooms to fight fires. Between times he looked after his ten-horse team, a harder chore than cooking. But his important chore remained cooking, for without "a good cook at the wagon they can't keep men."

Two of the more pleasantly remembered cooks were J. K. Marsh and Fred Graven, both of whom left accounts of their culinary experiences. Here is Marsh's story:

"The first of March, 1907, Rufe Morris' cook quit and I fell heir to the job. The XIT always put their extra men to work on the first of April, and about all they had to do was grease and mend harness, make tent pins out of ashwood, clean out the corrals, and there would be three men to one man's job for a few days. Rufe would start gathering saddle horses on the fifteenth of April, rain or shine, unless it happened to fall on *Friday*.

"It usually took about an hour to get breakfast after the

fire was started; so the cook was up fairly early. Steak, sour-dough bread, potatoes, and eggs (when we had them), butter, syrup, and Arbuckle coffee constituted breakfast. There was always dried fruit for those who liked it. For dinner there was roast or boiled beef, baked or boiled pota-toes, pie, pudding or son-of-a-gun in a sack (known to polite people as suet pudding) and whatever vegetables (out of a can of course) and sour-dough biscuits and coffee. Supper was steak, sour-dough biscuits, fried potatoes, some kind of canned vegetables, and dried fruit, and coffee. There was always meat and biscuits left over, and the cowboys were great hands to lunch between meals, which usually consisted of cold biscuits, meat, onions or pickles, and coffee. The coffeepot stayed hot all the time, especially in the spring and fall.

"When on the roundup the cook drove the mess wagon, the night hawk drove the bed wagon when they moved, and there was always a man sent along to pilot the wagons to the next camp ground, which, with the day horse wrangler, the four had to set up camp, which was sometimes quite a job if the wind was blowing hard.

"As soon as the tent was up, the stove had a fire in it and the coffeepot was put on. On the general roundup we hardly ever made but one move a day and rarely ever made but one roundup a day. But on the beef roundup we made one round-up and had supper early and moved out on the divide to grass after supper to a dry camp and moved back on the creek the next morning. For by fall there was not much grass along the creek bottom for the remuda and the beef herd, as the sheep camped along all summer."

Graven followed Marsh as a cook by two years, right at the close of the XIT's cattle-running days. His account is chiefly concerned with the making of sour-dough biscuits:

"In the spring of 1909 my old friend Charlie McNiel was over in Texas working for the XIT Ranch. He had married and they had given him the Rito Blanco headquarters in which to live. They wanted a wagon cook for the North Division of the XIT. They had a ranch cook, that previous to being with the ranch had been down in New Mexico in a logging camp, cooking. But he couldn't make sour-dough bread. If you can't make that kind of bread you will never make a chuck wagon cook. The Forest Service says that sour-dough bread is the most healthful bread in the world as a steady diet.

"My family were all cooks and I helped my sister, Mrs. Westmoreland. George showed me how to make sour-dough bread. There is something more to it than just stirring up flour and water. You get to know your dough just like a mechanic knows cars. You can't make sour-dough bread unless you have the right attitude of mind.

"When I first went to cooking for the XIT chuck wagon I used the potrack, but Bob Duke soon got me a camp stove. I could take it down at once and load it on the 'hoodlum wagon,' as the two-wheeled trailer behind was called. In baking sour-dough bread in this stove I always put a pan of water in the oven with it. Sour-dough bread must be baked with some moisture, which it naturally gets in a Dutch oven. I removed the pan of water from the oven before the bread was done to let it brown."

There is considerable argument throughout the reminiscences about who was the best cook. Mrs. C. R. Duke, a sister-in-law of our Mrs. Duke, holds out for Jim McLemore. Others suggest Lina Mims. Since none of the hands sampled the wares of all the cooks, it is impossible to assess one cook against another. Perhaps the consensus agrees with J. W. Standifer when he describes:

"Jim Perry, a Negro cook from Austin, Texas, and what a cook!* He could make the best son-of-a-gun I ever ate, and I never had a truer friend. He worked for the XIT off and on for twenty years. I once heard him say, 'If it weren't for my damned old black face I'd have been boss of one of these divisions long ago.' And he no doubt would have.

"He loved to dress up and go to town and show off before the other Negroes. He one time had a twenty-dollar hat. He wore it to Fort Worth and got mixed up with some city slicks. This other Negro told him he didn't want to be recognized in that part of town, and for them to exchange hats, but when the town Negro got his hand on Jim's twenty-dollar hat he skipped out, and that was the last of Jim's hat as far as he was concerned."

To this day survivors of the XIT continue to argue about which man was the best cook. So long as there are two survivors there will be no agreement, but for half a century most of the XIT men have concurred on one point: no one cooked son-of-a-gun stew or baked sour-dough biscuits like Goldie Thomas. Goldie himself thought he was good, and took the trouble to leave his recipes—or, more accurately, procedures, —to posterity. Here is how Goldie Thomas made the hands whoop with pleasure:

"There is just as much art in making sour-dough bread as a mechanic knowing where to start in on a car. You have to learn to know your dough.

"Now the first thing to do is get a pickle keg that has been well cleaned, size from one to five gallons, depending upon the amount of dough you want to make. With the

---

* W. T. Brown goes a step farther. Not only was Jim the best cook, but "the best Negro that ever lived," as well as the strongest and the best rider—"If they throwed me he would ride them for me."

wagon I used a five-gallon keg, say for ten or twelve men. I prefer a keg to anything else that you can use, because you just have better dough than you do when it is made up in crocks or other containers. All right, we have our keg ready now. Add as much water in the keg as you want dough to start with. Take one large Irish potato or two medium-size 'spuds,' as we always called them. Split the spuds lengthwise scraping the pulp into the keg. Add two tablespoons of sugar, then add a piece of yeast cake if you happen to have it—that makes the dough come up faster. Now add flour to make it a stiff batter. Then beat well and set in a warm place to rise.

"Now in starting a batch of dough I usually pour off the first one or two batches, leaving about a fourth of your dough in the keg, adding as much batter, that is flour and water, back in the keg as you poured off. When dough rises well up in the keg, your dough is ready to make biscuits. But don't ever let it come up and fall. If you are not ready to make bread when it comes up beat it down, and add a little more flour and let it come up again. Pour batter in which flour has been sifted. If dough is a little sour add a little soda, a pinch of sugar, and salt. Then knead flour into batter as for light rolls. Make out into biscuits, put into Dutch oven or deep pan which has been greased and let rise until they double their size and then cook slow for about three-fourths of an hour or until light brown. To make good son-of-a-gun use parts of a suckling calf, one that has not been weaned.

"I like to use a steel pot or a Dutch oven. I don't know why but is just seems to cook better. Try it in one. All right, we have our Dutch oven. Take a firm piece of tallow and cut up in very fine pieces, put it in pot, and render until tallow is almost brown. Then take the marrow-gut, cutting it to small pieces, then a heart-size piece of liver, sweetbreads, and small piece of kidney or using whole kidney and tongue, using a little meat also. The latter a piece off the neck is O.K., chopping up a few onions as to suit taste. Mix mare-hut, liver, sweetbreads, kidney, and a little chopped beef altogether. Add salt, pepper, and chili powder or pods to suit taste. Put these ingredients into hot tallow and let sear good and add water and let cook until tender. If your stew is a little thin add a little flour and water made into a batter with about ½ dozen eggs well beaten, stirring into batter. Then pour into pot, stirring briskly.

"Now *I would say that you have a real son-of-a-gun.*"

Thomas also explained why his coffee invariably suited:

"We had our coffee mill fastened right on to the chuck box, then sometimes we had to parch our coffee and grind it. It seemed as if it had a better flavor. The first thing is to have the coffeepot good and clean, as we always washed ours after each meal. Having a two-gallon pot three-fourths filled with water with one-half pound of ground coffee. I always put coffee and water in pot and let set over night and set on the fire the following morning and let *simmer* but *never boil.* Boiling ruins coffee. Try this and I think you will have good coffee."

A strong case could be made that the chuck wagon cook was the most important man in the XIT or any other outfit, but the same case could be made for any other hand. But in a negative sense he was the most important man, for he was the one man who in an instant could demoralize a camp by turning out bitter coffee, tasteless biscuits, and insipid stew.

But he'll move when it's mud t' the axles;
　An' he'll put up his tent in a storm.
An' he'll fix up hot coffee, an' move things around,
　T' let the boys in t' git warm.
An' he don't never need any pilot,
　F'r he knows the whole range like a book.

So he works when he wants to, r' quits and gits drunk
F'r the onery ol' buzzard c'n cook.*

* From "The Round-Up Cook," by Jim Fisher, an XIT poet. Published by permission of *The Cattleman*, XIX (September, 1932), 21.

THE OTHER SIDE
OF THE DRAW

NONE OF THE INVESTORS in the Capitol Freehold Land and Investment Company, Limited, ever had much notion of putting his boots or brogans through a pair of levis, fastening chaps, knotting his neckerchief, or pulling his grease-spotted sombrero low over his forehead and mounting a mustang to become a working cowhand on the XIT. Least of all were the Farwells of Chicago attracted to everyday ranch life, except as it could be entered on a statement of profit and loss. Of the original pair, Charles B. Farwell was a congressman, and later senator, who nursed hopes of being

President some day; while John V. Farwell was one of Chicago's solid "merchant princes," deviating from his fellow royalty only in his devotion to religious work. It was John V. Farwell who helped organize the first YMCA in the world and promoted a Chicago youth named Dwight L. Moody, and preached with the great revivalist in Union Army camps and in the British Isles. He did spend some time on the ranch, holding church services as one of his pursuits.

But a member of the second generation of Farwells did take sufficient interest in the ranch of his father and uncle that he finally moved to the ranch to live for several years. When Walter Farwell learned that Mrs. Duke was collecting reminiscences he sent along his. The portion that follows gives a picture from the other side of the draw:

"We drove over the prairie, flat as a floor, and with nothing to obstruct the view save an occasional soapweed or cactus. The horizon seemed a long way off, and it was, for the automobile had not yet arrived. Curiously enough one seemed to be always driving up a slight incline, probably some trick of air refraction. However, the light air was always crisp and agreeable.

"One day we turned up at Buffalo Springs, where at the time we were conducting one of the first farming experiments in the Panhandle. Riding and roping was a part of the game, but plowing and digging postholes went hard with the adventurous spirit of the old-time cowboy. Among the outfit was Ab Owings, tall, raw-boned, burnt yellow by the sun, and with a habit of riding sideways in the saddle, acquired by long days on the trail. One of the tasks was painting a barn with Owings as foreman. When the job was done it was found that all the pigs on the place had been roped and a white circle painted around their tails. Actions speak louder than words.

"This was only one of the many visits I made to the ranch.

About 1904 I was at Bovina at the time of the Great Blizzard. Arriving at the ranch house I was greeted by long rows of fresh hides stretched on the fences to dry. The snow had been on the ground for sixty days, and cottonseed cake was a poor substitute for grass. As we drove about the pastures with John Armstrong, the division foreman, we were never out of sight of dead cattle. Every once in a while good old John would get out, 'tail-up' some weak fallen animal, and give it a new chance for life. That year brought heavy cattle losses at Bovina and was anything but agreeable. It took an effort to remember other occasions when, on the green hills of Montana, I had ridden through herds of heavy beef steers munching the tall grama grass and ready to top the market at Kansas City or Chicago.

"That same winter Joe Frazier, division foreman, George Findlay, from the Chicago office, and I drove across from Hereford to the Escarbada Ranch. We could not wait for the weather, though there was a cold blizzard blowing from the north. When we left town we had no roads and could see only a hundred feet ahead, for the air was full of snow.

" 'How do you know where you are going,' I asked Joe. 'I should think you would be lost.'

"Joe was annoyed.

" 'Lost,' he repeated. 'All you got to do is to watch the way the wind blows the grass.'

"Apparently anything is easy if you only know how. Driving along in that norther, though with heavy coats and jugs of hot water between our feet, we were chilled to the bone, and a much desired drink of raw liquor on reaching the ranch tasted like water. I thought with envy of Mrs. Farwell, who that winter was cruising on a yacht on the sunny blue waters of the Mediterranean.

"Becoming more occupied with ranch affairs, Mrs. Far-

well* and I did over an old farm house on the outskirts of
Channing and lived there for several years. Much land was
being sold and the herds were being reduced to comply with
the smaller acreage, but we were not always busy. Every once
in a while we would ride to a nearby outfit to have dinner at
the wagon, or over the hills for a visit to old Tascosa. On
special occasions we gave dances, attended by cowboys from
far and near. Any morning we might wake up and find some
unexpected rancher friend asleep in our guest room. The
trains seldom arrived anywhere except in the middle of the
night and by no possible chance were they ever on time. No
one seemed to care; the days never seemed too long.

"A good many years have gone by and life to many of
us is now one of meditation rather than action. Just the same
it is a compensation to have known the Panhandle at the turn
of the century, when the frontier was free and unregenerate,
with civilization and decorum still in the future. Another
compensation, and a far greater, is the friends that one made.
Cowboys or ranchmen, stirring days produced sterling men,
and it is a privilege to have known them."

Although Walter Farwell does not receive a single negative
vote from any XIT cowboy who left his recollections, he had
one penchant that the men would have preferred unindulged.

"Walter Farwell was great on playing polo and had a polo
field south of Channing. He was always looking for good
cow horses, good at cutting out and roping, to take back east
to use in polo. They learned the game quickly.

"The boys did not like for their good night horses to go

* One XIT hand who never forgot Mrs. Farwell was A. L.
Denby. He was cooking when she came into the kitchen to meet
him. "After we had chatted a few minutes she pulled out her ciga-
rettes and offered them to me. You could have knocked my eyes off
with a stick, as I wasn't used to seeing ladies smoke."

back east and have their legs beat up with polo sticks. Some of the boys would teach their horses to pitch or buck every time Mr. Farwell came near the wagon. Others hid their horses in the canyons or tried to do so, and as every man was with them in this, they were not to be found, not even by the good little horse wrangler Hondo."*

When A. G. Boyce decided to retire after nearly two decades as general manager of the XIT, he was replaced by H. S. Boice, a quiet, praying man with a will like a rock. It was his job to preside over the final liquidation of XIT cattle. But before that last day came, he continued to make the raising and selling of cattle for profit his chief concern. To insure the proper functioning of his still vast enterprise, he demanded regular reports from his division foremen. Three letters, two short and one longer, all from R. L. Duke, give an idea of the variety of problems encountered. The first was written on September 14, 1906:

"Dear Mr. Boice: I come in last night to try to talk to you, but come a rain in the night so cannot get anyone over the phone. I will come back tonight after we brand if it dries up so I can talk over the phone. Florence is starting down to Rito Blanco this afternoon. Will come to Channing Saturday to see you in regards to the land he has. I will enclose letter from Jess Morris in regards to land he has in Agua Frio Pasture. This land is on east side next to fence. It shows on the map in the Agua Frio Pasture. The Company has had it leased ever since he has had the land. . . .

"I will get done branding here Sunday night, round up shipping pasture Monday, and start to Perico Tuesday with

* Hondo was not known for his learning. But despite his inability to count beyond his ten fingers, he would invariably bring in every last horse of a remuda, that usually ran between 125 and 150.

herd. Calf crop is short here, same as Rito Blanco. I fear it is going to be short everywhere.

"Has the pine tar, acid, and turpentine been ordered for Dr. Netherton? I do not know how much he will want. I do not think we will have over fourteen hundred calves to spay. I shipped what I had left of pine tar, turpentine to John Armstrong last spring. I probably have a gallon of each, not over that. So please order it for me so it will be at Perico the twenty-third.

"Cattle is doing good here, as below. I will write you when I get done, if I can't talk to you, and send you tallies of each pasture.

"I ordered two barrels of mineral red and linseed oil for Perico. See if you can get the people at the store to rush it up, as the boys at Buffalo Springs is moving nicely and do not want them to run out of paint, as they have got their work under headway. Also send me six gallons of white and the green to trim the places up there.

R. L. Duke"

Two days later Duke was writing again, this time at more length:

"Dear Mr. Boice: I finished branding here today, as I intended. Will round up herd tomorrow to start to Perico Tuesday morning. The worst part of this whole thing is that I put the herd that I brought from Rito Blanco in shipping pasture here till I worked this range, and the gate was left open the same as last spring, only a different gate and let these cattle back in the JJ Range. They were found, and instead of letting me know about it they turned 182 head into Pederosa right back where I brought them from. Now I hafto go back there to get this stuff, and of course will hafto work the pasture to do it, but I cannot think of going off and

leaving these cattle, for there was a quite a few of them
steers, and the balance was old cows that I had cut for beef.
I am sending a few men back to gather them while I go ahead
with the rest. This knocks my plans endways. Anyway I will
be ready for the doctor just the same. While I will not be able
to have the full crew there for two or three days, but we
will handle them as fast as the doctor will turn them loose.
Owing to this delay it will delay my work up there some.
Will say about five days.

"Please let me know just what time you have ordered
cars, for if the doctor could spay them out we are in shape to
brand out 600 a day, which would be 500 heifers a day, but
I am sure he will not run them out that fast. If he puts out
200 a day he will do well as it will take half of the day to
round them up. When I see how fast he can put them out I
will write you. I think we will have about 3,000 calves up
here. They ought to average about 1500 heifers. I took something like 300 from here last spring, the bad colors to Rito
Blanco. I have gathered about 500 fat cows here and at Rito
Blanco besides the bunch I taken up last spring, which is in
South Carrizo Pasture. Two-year-old steers will be put in
Perico Pasture. I enclose number of calves branded to date,
and all Buffalo Springs is to brand yet. Cattle looks good as
can be expected,

Yours truly,
R. L. Duke"

The second shorter report was written the following
summer:

"Dear Mr. Boice:
As I can't get you by phone, I have worked on this box
and it rings light and clear here. I am leaving word for Jim
to take his test phone and come over it Monday till he meets

Ed. I think when we find this trouble it will be as last year—someone has put a ground on it by a post somewhere as it worked the same as then. I look for Frank Jackson to come in there Monday. If he does I want him to come on to Perico, get a horse there, and come on the West Middle Water Pasture and meet us. We will be working in the creek somewhere near Mill No. 25 just below Bull Pasture fence. He can come to Camp Repentance and will find us.

R. L. Duke"

FROLICKING

FRED GRAVEN could spell, and he knew something about grammar. Although he was a good hand on a ranch, everywhere he went throughout the Panhandle he was asked to quit his cowpunching and turn schoolmaster. The reason was that nearly every school ma'am that came into the area soon married a ranchman.* Women were scarce in this man's world, and single women of courting size almost nonexistent. Or so it seemed.

The scarcity of women is indicated by the experience of Mrs. Allen Willbanks, who had been gently reared back in

---

* Graven, incidentally, never taught. He writes: "Me? I wouldn't teach, not in a house."

settled, semi-Southern Johnson County, Texas, and had joined her husband in the spring of 1901 while he drilled wells for the XIT. During the remainder of spring and through the summer, the young couple, with their infant daughter, Stella, had lived in a tent, slept on the ground, sat on wire spools for chairs, eaten off goods boxes from tin cups and tin plates, and cooked with cow chips. After a short stay in Channing, where Mrs. Willbanks had given birth to and buried a baby boy, they had moved back into a camp east of Dalhart.

"I did not see a lady that whole year, and I did not see but two ladies the next year; one of these ladies ate dinner with us. [Tobe Pitts' wife] and one other lady passed along in about one-half mile of our camp."

Mrs. Willbanks had whiled away her time by helping her husband, playing with Stella, keeping camp, and washing white little-girl dresses that she hung on sage or bear grass or on guy wires connected to the well rig.

"We had lots of fun, we made fun out of our work."

Actually, although the proportion of females to males was a bit dismal from both a woman's and a man's standpoint, the XIT country had enough "girls there and some coming in now and then" to dangle the promise of spice and perfume, and once in a while to give the hands an excuse to slick down their hair with water and go calling. And any cowboy who spent a year on the ranch was going to be invited to at least one whing-ding of a ball during that time that would leave him with memories of flashing eyes and whirling skirts to liven up the lonely hours at a line camp later. It might, as Gene Elliston suggests, require all the girls between Amarillo and Trinidad, Colorado, to have a dance, but nonetheless the balls came off periodically. From time to time even the Texline courthouse was converted into a dance hall.

Most of the time, however, complains J. S. Kenyon, he

spent his nights lying on buffalo or mesquite grass "looking up at the beautiful stars. It would make any of us think poetry . . . about the moon kissing us, about the only way any of us ever got any kisses." But Kenyon didn't spend all his time with Keats, his favorite poet. In 1886 he attended a dance "in the Curtis hollow on Catfish Creek in the Two Buckle Ranch pasture," along with three other hands off the Spur Ranch. The quartet "had two horses hitched to the front wheels of the wagon and sat on it. The gentle sex were few in number at the dance, only three young married women. Two men had to dance together to make up a set. I had a pretty good time, as I was only a kid and the others were about thirty year old. On our way back across the prairie no road. My party got a little too much fire water.* I was driving to suit them, fast, and we sailed off a bluff about ten feet high into a ravine in the prairie. Fortunately it had a sandy bottom. None of us were hurt, but they let me regulate the speed thereafter.

"I went to a dance at Merkel in 1885. There was enough girls—two sets—I had a good time. I must say the women and girls treated me very nicely in Texas and I have always remembered them with much pleasure. Miss Mattie Middleton and Miss Purcell, originally South Carolina families. Miss Mattie filled an old widower that night with candy and crackers. He went from one to another holding his hat behind him in his hand. Whenever Miss Mattie passed she dropped candy or crackers in his hat."

The girls were as eager for the dances as the cowboys. Ina Chillcut recalls that girl friends of hers from as far away as Trinidad, Colorado, and Clarendon, Texas, would manage to visit her if a dance was in prospect.

* Writes Gene Elliston: "Cowpunchers always drinks the bad whiskey first—then it is all good."

"We girls would help the boys mow the hay—do anything to get through—have supper, and go to the bunkhouse to dance. The boys were from every walk of life, the educated and the uneducated, but were equal as cowboys, . . . Once we had a dancing master, who also played the violin; he taught us many steps. We not only danced at the ranch, but would hitch a team to the hack and go thirty-one miles to Clayton, New Mexico, to dances. Sometimes we would go to Texline, leave the team, go up on the train, come back, get the team, and go back to the ranch. Usually the girls were going home when we did this."

One reason why everyone liked to go to Clayton was that it was a great sheep headquarters with a high per capita proportion of gamblers, a turn-of-the-century equivalent of a sin city. Also it was a gathering place for Mexicans, and, in Mrs. Chillcut's words, "If you never danced a Mexican quadrille, get some one to teach you how. The most beautiful dance yet. Ten-twenty or thirty couples can dance it or as many as the hall will hold."

At one of the XIT dances Mrs. Duke's sister met her future husband—also a Duke. As she remembers it, she visited our Mrs. Duke often on her homestead north of Buffalo Springs across the line in Oklahoma.

"From her dugout on the claim we had a good view of Buffalo Springs, which consisted of several red barns and corrals and a white house surrounded by trees and a stone house [cook's house], bunkhouse, and other small buildings. But what looked the best of all to us was the trees growing up and down the creek, because trees in that part of the Panhandle were few and far between.

"Mr. and Mrs. Corder were cooking there at that time. They decided to have a dance at the Springs. . . . We went, and it was a momentous occasion for me, as I met my future husband there that night, C. R. Duke, an XIT cowboy. He came up and introduced himself and asked me to waltz with him. I guess he liked my looks as well as I liked him, because I have been married to him now for twenty-six years and I still think the XIT cowboys are a fine lot of men.

"The XIT cowboys always wore dancing shoes,* and we danced in a room about fourteen by sixteen. Everyone came to the ranch in a wagon or buggy. . . . There were not very many women and girls there, and not a bobbed head in the bunch. Most of them wore their hair in the latest pompadour, and curled their own hair by heating the curlers over a coal-oil lamp. Our dresses almost touched the floor and were tight as beeswax. Lipstick, rouge, and permanents were unknown.

"We danced the schottische, waltz, glide polka, and all kinds of square dances. We waltzed to the tune of 'Good-Bye Old Paint' until the early hours of the morning. Mr. and Mrs. Corder served us a twelve-o'clock supper, cake and coffee, the best I ever tasted.

"The music was a couple of fiddles. . . . Everyone from the Oklahoma side of the line pronounced it the best dance they ever attended.

" 'Those were the good old days.' "

But the girls weren't the only ones who would ride all day to dance the night away. J. K. Marsh admits that at the XIT spread in Montana the hands often "had to go anywhere from twenty to sixty miles to get crowd enough for a dance, and when we got there we danced as much as sixteen hours. I have known when a blizzard came up, that where the dance was at an out-of-the-way ranch, the whole crowd stayed three days and would dance and sleep away the time. The great trouble was to find room to bed down everybody, but

---

* Mrs. Duke says that never in her life did she see a cowboy dance with his spurs on, and that "any cowboy with spurs on would have been called off the floor."

there was always plenty to eat, as all the married women always brought plenty of cakes.

"The big dances of the winter were at the Hamelow Ranch on Tusler Creek, John Buttleman's on Bad Route, Cracker Box Pete's [Pete Evans] on Cracker Box, Kiney's on the Yellowstone. . . . Ed and Louis Weisner were violinists and worked for the XIT. They played for all of the dances and would go horseback with their fiddles tied on their backs. Most of the time we took up a dollar from each man to pay for the music, and the rule was that the musicians got the collection whatever it might be. But toward the last the ranchers got so they insisted that they were giving the dance and intended to pay for it.

". . . [In] December 1907 . . . we had a big farewell dance . . . at the Hatchett Ranch. The Yellowstone was late freezing that year and Ed Weisner kept the ferry in on purpose for the dance. The people from the south side came over early in the afternoon, but it got pretty cold that night and the slush ice was running so thick the next morning that neither rowboat nor ferry could run. So we just kept on dancing, as the slush did not run out until late in the afternoon so there was a possibility of getting across. All of the men went to the ferry and helped get the boat across with the people in it, and then we came back in row boats and had a hard time getting back."

Probably the most sought-after dancer around the Montana spread was Mrs. H. J. Kramer of Fallon, whose husband accompanied the trains of XIT cattle to Chicago every autumn. Mrs. Kramer loved to waltz and taught many a cowpuncher how to count "one-two-three." Besides, as one points out, "she was a large strong lady who could steer them around."

Sometimes, when no women were available, the cowboys would throw their own bunkhouse "shindig" just to break

the monotony of looking at each other. J. W. Standifer tells
about one such party in which several Negroes took part
while the other hands looked on and shouted encouragement.
Their particular favorite was an old Negro named Big Joe,
whose real fame came neither from his cowpunching nor
his sideline of banjo-picking, but from a pair of the most
enormous feet any of the other cowhands had ever laid eyes
on. Big Joe's feet got that way from going barefoot all summer. He even rode barefoot.

Perhaps not too strangely the XIT cowboys' reminiscences
say almost nothing about red-light houses or their "soiled
dove" denizens. The only real mention, and it is only a
mention, comes from the effervescent Gene Elliston's account
of his arrival in the Panhandle.*

"It was in the spring of 1892 I landed in Tascosa on the
night train. The depot was on the south of the Canadian
River, the town on the north side about one and one-half
miles apart. So old Pap Price, as we called him, ran a bus
from town to depot to haul mail and passengers.

"That night a pal of mine, myself, and nine jolly red-
light girls was passengers on the bus. It was a jolly crowd and
all lit up with snake whiskey and smothering it with cigarette
smoke. We rolled along over to town. When we reached
town one of the girls said, 'Kid,' addressing me, 'What are
you going to do here?' I said, 'I don't know. I am looking for
work.' She said, 'Come go with me tonight and I will show
you a time, will put you on the road to prosperity.' By that
time we had got on to the hotel. My pal and I got out. The
balance of the bunch went on whooping and yelling to the
dance hall.

"Old Monichy Russell was running the hotel—he called

* Elliston apologizes for his inability to write formal, stilted
English: "I never went through but one grammar and was looking for pictures, then found none. I quit grammar."

it the Annex. Monichy was an old Bar E cowpuncher and
freight boss . . . , a great character, big-hearted, fine fellow
but rough as you make them."

Since many of the people in the XIT area had come out of
the Old South, or at least from an Old South heritage, July 4
did not especially appeal to them as a day for celebration. But
after General Joe Wheeler, who as a twenty-six–year–old
brigadier had made a name for himself at Shiloh and elsewhere, carved a new reputation for himself as a general of
cavalry in the Spanish War at the end of the century, the
Panhandle folk decided to rejoin the Union in enthusiasm
as well as in political allegiance. Besides, many of Theodore
Roosevelt's Rough Riders had come off the ranches of Oklahoma, Texas, and New Mexico. And so in 1900 the XIT
boys decided to have a big July 4 picnic on Hackberry Creek,
a running-water stream east of the Cold Water Draw. In Fred
Graven's words, they "would do things up brown, no half-
hearted business."

"They had a big barbecue in which beef played the main
part. This with bread, pickles, and coffee enough to last
three days: 3, 4 and 5 July. They expected everybody in a
hundred miles. They had a 'stand' that sold ice cream and
lemonade—the first ice cream some of the children had ever
seen.

"The fireworks were in a wagon bed, and two cowboys
who were working for the picnic with more zeal than knowl-
edge started them in the middle of the afternoon. In their
excitement they dropped lighted matches in the wagon-bed
among the fireworks. A few of the firecrackers went off themselves, then the whole works went to shooting off in all directions. The cowboys had their pant legs on fire; they ran
to the creek. Everybody ran for the creek, which had high
banks, but they jumped over them. They had trench warfare
for a while with the fireworks for the enemy. They all had

room to run; in fact, the farther they ran the more room they had.

"A horse got scared along with them, grazing near the center of the picnic ground. He ran, too, over the bank, but he landed in one of the deep holes and he couldn't get out, as the steep banks went down in the water for five or six feet. They lassooed him by the horn on the saddle. Some one shouted 'You'll pull that horn off!' But the men all got hold of the rope as they do in these county fair 'tug o' wars' and pulled him out by the horn of the saddle.

"The barbecue pits and the 'stand' were away at one side; so the people near them had a good view of the fireworks. Some range cattle that had been looking at them from the nearby hills, they lit out, too. These human beings were past finding out.

"Nobody was killed and nobody was hurt; so they all went to the dance platform and began the square dances. They had one change in the set, as it is called, and they were saying 'Honor your pardners and promenade back. First couple out' when one man on the set, a well-known cowman, was showing unmistakable evidence of having something stronger to drink than coffee. His wife come out of the crowd and walked straight across the platform. The dance stopped in spite of the caller. She walked up to him—she was taller than he was—took him by the ear, and led him off.

"Did he go? He went like a sheep-killing dog.

"Then some of the men began to look for this drink stronger than coffee. There was a deaf-and-dumb boy, a relative of Charley Hitch. This boy had been given some, and he was making noises that were fearful indeed. They couldn't stop him. So they took him up the creek a half mile or so and tied him to a tree. One boy stayed and watched him. They took turns until a shower came up [with] keen lightning. They took him home.

"They knew this stuff was not in No-Man's-Land, neither did it come down from dry Kansas. It had to come up from Texas. They found who brought it up, a friend of this well-known cowman. So they got it and poured it in a spring hole.

"Everybody had come with bedrolls and were prepared to camp. On the fifth they all started home. They had had plenty of food, had seen their old friends, had kept law and order, and all went home happy."

There were, of course, other ways of having fun than stomping the boards. Cowboy kangaroo courts are notorious, and the XIT hands held their share until, as Lee Landers remembers it, they tried a visiting Englishman one bitter cold day. Found guilty of something or other, the visitor started backing up in the face of punitive threats from his judges. Finally he backed into a stock tank "and nearly froze to death." The boss, J. E. Moore, ordered an end to such trials.

Practical jokes and teasing, about as unsubtle as barbed wire, were frequent. One favorite trick was to wait till some snowy night, drag a line across an occupied bedroll, and yell "Rattlesnake!" Half the hands would be on their feet shaking off the dread serpent before they realized that the weather was too cold for rattlesnakes to be abroad.

Considerable levity could be worked up from luring a tenderfoot astride an outlaw or from watching one hand work rings around another. The XIT did not permit drinking or gambling on its premises, though undoubtedly some of both took place. Certainly, once they were away from the reservation the XIT men were as eager for high jinks as any other cowboy or sailor or miner isolated for months from the dubious delights of some half-formed town. *

* Mrs. Willbanks tells of attending a celebration in Clayton where the sport was to bury a chicken in the ground. Then each cowboy made a run and grabbed at it. When the riders "finely" pulled the chicken out of the ground they began shooting at each other, ap-

Some diversions were not exactly in the fun category. Whenever men were thrown together for as long as these cowboys were, with little break in their routine, quarrels and feuds were bound to develop. Sometimes the friction merely grew out of a contest of wills, one man's opinion against another's, and represented no more than that. But then again the friction might develop into real heat, with someone getting hurt. One suspects that the cowboys weren't above "egging on" the contenders in a first-class fuss, just to have something to watch and to talk about.

Most of the men who rose to any sort of foreman level climbed there because they knew how to take charge. Because they were natural leaders, they made and carried out their decisions with a confidence that on occasion could border on pure mulishness. Although Frank Yearwood was one of the more highly respected XIT foremen, both while he was operating and in retrospect, on at least one occasion he locked horns with a hand and came out second-best. Lewis Derrick, the hand in question, tells about it:

"So Yearwood was the boss and he said we would go to Spring Lake. He was riding his pet horse, Rustler by name. Said he would take us to camp. So we rode for a long time and hadn't got off the Bend country. I told one of the boys we were millin'. So he and I stopped pretty soon. They came around a sand hill, and we hollered at them and Frank says, 'Who air you?'

"Well, we guide them a while and he would not try to go. Anyway, I was camped ten miles south of Spring Lake and was riding a horse that me and Ames Simpson had him running races on and I told the bunch if they would not crowd me I believed my horse would go to my camp, but if they

crowded me he would want to run and if they didn't let him
run, he would prance and would not go nowhere. So Frank
told me to pull out. So I did, and I told him just keep clost
enough to see me. The boss said I going straight as a die.

"So we rode for some time, got off the burn, and they got
off a gag that they wanted to tell me. So the boss and one of
the boys run up on each side of me, and I held my horse and
would not let them run, and he rared and fretted, and I got
hard-boiled and gave them pretty good cussing, for I was
cold. The boss was the only one that had a coat and overshoes.
So boss said we stay right there till daylight. When daylight
come Frank ask the bunch the way to camp. I pointed northeast and the rest pointed southwest. I told them I could not
leave them in snowstorm, but they would go into Mexico.
So we pulled out southwest late in the eavening. They struck
a road. The snow was thin enough that we could see the trails.
So the boss asked me where that road went. I told them that
right hand would go to Salt Lake and the left would go to
Yellow Houses and 'you air still crazy.'

"He said, 'maybe crazy as hell, but I am going to the ranch
and get some chuck. You fellers can go on southwest.' So I
started and Nigger Jo said, 'I'll follow Mister Lewis.' We go
a mile before they decided to follow us.

"When they caught up we were going in the gate at the
Silver Lake Pasture."

A more serious quarrel with near-fatal consequences developed while S. R. Cooper worked for the Spring Lake Division in 1890. Cooper, who describes himself as "no smart-
er than the law will allow" but only a "lover of good people
and of honest people," has a way with the written word that
is at once original and confusing. If in reading his account
of the following fight you lose control of the narrative and
don't always know which is which or who is fighting whom,
you have the company of this editor!

"My last day and night on the XIT was a pretty hot day. I had been rustling prairie coal* and was not at the branding pen when the trouble come up, but two of the boys, one I think was twenty-four and the other one I judge was about thirty-five, had a quarrel in the branding pen and still felt a little ruffled when they came to the chuck wagon that night. As it happened both of their beds and mine had been thrown on the north side of the chuck wagon and all the other boys' beds had been thrown on the south side of it, and I had left my chip or prairie-coal wagon east of the chuck wagon.

"Now you may wonder why I remember so well just how things were placed. Well, I'll tell you, I never had seen men fight before. The cook had supper ready. The camp fire on the south side of the wagon where most of the beds were. We all ate supper and talked a while, and as I was tired I went around the chuck wagon and fixing to crawl into bed. And the twenty-four–year came around to his bed, but he had before that slipped the boss's Winchester out of the chuck wagon, placed it under the head of his bed. Soon after, C, thirty-five. Then the thirty-five came around and renewed their trouble. Their beds were only a few feet apart. C drawed the gun from his bed—it still in the scabbard—and drawed it like he intended to use it as a club but soon drawed it from the scabbard and cocked it.

"I was not feeling very safe but stayed with my bed and my close were still on and I left them on. Perry kept stepping up closer to Clem and finely Clem turned and ran around the chip wagon and taken the gun with him, and hollered to Perry not to come around there. Perry had a long-bladed pocket knife, but it was then dark and no one seemed to know he had it but the man he borrowed it from. So some of the boys went to Clem and got him to give up the gun and

* This is not the same coal that is mined in Pennsylvania.

then hollered to Perry to come on as Clem had given up his gun and would fight him a fair fist fight. So Perry went around there, and all the rest of us to see the fight, and some boys standing between them stepped back to let them together.

"Clem made a dive for Perry's legs, aiming to tip him over, but Perry doubled over him and caught under Clem's stomach with his left hand and began using his knife with the right hand, stabbing Clem in the back and left side close to his short ribs and we soon began to hear the blood gush, and one of the boys said, 'Pull them apart—Perry has a knife!' And an old man—I do not remember his name, they called him uncle—he grabbed Perry and told him to quit using that knife, and some of the others got a hold and pulled them apart.

"I took Clem back to his bed and let him lay with his left side down so it would let the blood drain out but Clem seemed to think he would pass out. But in a short time Perry came around to his bed. They spatted a while, but Clem told Perry, 'I am in no shape to fight you, and about killed.' Perry said he ought to have cut his heart out.

"So things quieted down for the night, but very early the next morning all were up except Clem, and he was not so bad off as he thought he was. They harnessed up the chuck-wagon team, which was a small team of wiry mules, to take Clem to Canyon to a doctor, and as I had seen about all the wildness and tried to make a hand on a big cow ranch about as long as I care to, I went to the boss and called for my check and saddled up one of Clem's horses and led the other one—my bed on it—and drove day and night. Just stopped and let the mules and horses graze a little, and hook, and saddle up, and move on.

"Clem stood the trip pretty well, but I'm sure he never forgot what happened on the XIT Ranch. I saw the boss,

Frank Yearwood, in Amarillo about a month later and he told me that Clem got along all O.K. but did not come back to the ranch."

A more innocent type of pleasure, if the foregoing can be considered pleasure, came from exchanging yarns—spinning them, with here and there a little embroidery. J. S. Standifer tells how Allie Hondo, the little Mexican wrangler, was preparing one day to kill a beef. He had tied the cow to a fence and was poised to knock it in the head with an ax. But somehow he became entangled in the rope, the cow jerked Hondo's feet out from under him, and the Mexican stood completely on his head "for what seemed like a minute." When everyone teased him, Hondo shouted angrily, "One time laugh, all right; allie time laugh, too damn much."

Another of Standifer's yarns went like this:

"Boyce was a fine manager and made lots of money for the Syndicate, and also a fine man but a hard one to work for—you worked both early and late and Sunday as well as Monday. He told this one himself. Said one time Ira Aten, foreman of Division 5, had gathered a certain bunch of cattle and cut part of it to go to market. And in some fashion or other they got the orders mixed and Aten turned the wrong herd loose. Boyce, being a very blustery man, simply went up in the air about it. Aten was also rather high-strung. Boyce threatened to fire Aten, and Aten said: 'All right, I'll be damn glad of it. I'll go work for a man that will let me go to Sunday School.' "

Blue Stevens liked to tell of a joke he played on Hooly Ann ["Julian," in Spanish] Menzor, a broncobuster for the Buffalo Springs Division. Stevens was his herder.

"His bronc trotted ahead of me. I slipped my rope under his tail. Say, cowboy, you should have seen that bronc pitch. I roped the bronc and brought him back to the rider. [Hooly

Ann] said, 'Blue, what did you do to that bronc?' I said, 'Nothing,' which in cowboy pranks is the best to say."

Bob Beverly had a friend and coworker named Dick Estes. The pair were working together, handling mules, one of which had never been either bridled or unbridled without being tied down. Dick didn't approve of such coddling. He jerked the bridle off fractious Findlay, got away with it, and staked the old gray mule out for the night. During the night it rained, soaking the stake rope and leaving it as hard as iron.

The next morning Beverly told Dick not to stretch his luck with Findlay. But Dick led the mule beside his mate, "reached back and taken hold of the bridle, put the bits in the mule's mouth, and went to pull the headstall up over the mule's ears." Then the real Findlay took over.

"Old Findlay slung his head down and hit Dick in the stomach, knocking Dick down, and as he rose from the ground, he had hold of one of the ropes with an iron pin on the end of it. He swung the rope around and hit old Findlay on top of the head. The mule fell like he had been shot. Dick jumped on him, turned his head up, and hollered to me to hand him the bridle. Old Findlay just rung his tail one time and stiffened out dead. I said, 'You have killed our lead mule.' Dick said, 'I don't give a d——. This Syndicate outfit has got two million dollars to buy mules that a fellow can bridle.' "

That night the pair returned to camp. Beverly had four mules pulling his wagon, but Estes had only three.

"Dick told the boss about old Findlay eating so much corn that it killed him. Us XIT cowpunchers had to hang together, or we would have hung separately."

Beverly was also full of tales about the tightest cow-puncher ever to ride for the XIT. Here are just a few:

"When we reached the ranch there was an old fellow who gave his name as James ——— that had a photo outfit and a gramophone with tubes to place in your ears, and he would let us listen with tubes in our ears for five cents apiece. Of course we all listened to the tunes, that is, all of us but Byron Morris. He never spent any money in his life that I know of.

"One time Dick Estes, Jim Anderson, Emmett Hall, and I tried to take him to Clayton to a Mexican *bailey* or 'biley.'* We got him out of the pasture about four or five miles. Byron broke away from us and we run him about ten miles, trying to rope his horse, but he was riding a better horse than the rest of us, and besides he was light and just outrode us.

"That fall the Rock Island built into Liberal, Kan., and we went over there to ship and Byron bought a nickel's worth of chewing gum and divided with the outfit.

"Byron saved his first checks, tied up in a piece of old slicker or oilcloth until Mr. Boyce and the bookkeeper had to make him turn the checks in so they could account to the Company for them and he loaned the money to McMasters at Channing Mercantile, and after he found out he could draw interest on his money he never spent anything hardly for clothing or eats. He was a very peculiar fellow but never bothered about anyone else's business. Old man Cato, on the XIT Montana ranch called Byron one of Boyce's bee hunters."

Even the administration got in on some of the yarns. As a boy Walter Farwell, of the second generation of the family that founded the XIT, came down with his father, his uncle, Colonel Abner Taylor, Henry Stephens (another uncle), and A. G. Boyce. The group inspected one division headquarters after another. In the 1880's the herds were being gathered, not improved, and Farwell remembers those early herds look-

* Baile, or dance.

ing like an aurora borealis, making up in color and in length of horn what they lacked in weight and beef and breeding.

Eventually the party arrived at Yellow Houses, where they found Phelps White, a veteran ranchman, scarred from a nearly fatal prairie fire. After supper they sat smoking on the veranda. One of the Chicagoans had the poor taste to suggest to White that the Panhandle ought to make good sheep and goat country.

"To White, like all cattlemen, the mere name of sheep was war.

" 'Hell,' he exclaimed, 'sheep are no good and goats are worse. I can get you all you want for $2.50 a head.'

"Colonel Taylor, a Kentuckian, understood poker if he knew little of goats. 'All right,' he said, 'I'll take that bet. I'll buy all you like at that price.'

"White smiled a little quizzically. 'O.K., Colonel,' he agreed, 'don't forget that's a bargain.'

"Several days passed and we were back again at the ranch. The outfit was in and we had dinner at the wagon: chili con-carne, mashed potatoes cooked with onions, hot biscuits, and strong black coffee. Someone happened to look up and no-ticed a small cloud of dust rising over the hills just back of camp. It was a perfectly clear day, no clouds anywhere, and the sight occasioned some surprise. However, it came nearer and was accompanied by the rumble of many feet. At last emerging from the dust appeared a number of goats, the vanguard of a herd of at least a couple of thousand. White came to life with a slow grin and turned to Colonel Taylor.

" 'There are your goats, Colonel,' he said. 'What do you want done with them?'

"The joke was on the Colonel, but I cannot recall whether he compromised the deal or had them shipped to Kansas City for speculation."

The sister of Tobe Pitts, who later became Ina Chillcut,

was something of a goat fancier herself, but strictly for pets. Sometimes her goats became nuisances for other than the usual reasons. For one thing, in cold weather they would crawl atop the sleeping cattle to get warm. Up would come the cows and off would go the goats, bleating angrily. Sometimes they would jump from the cows' backs to the corral fence, only to find their positions worsened—and the infernal noise would intensify. One of Ina's goats, however, became something of a favorite for his sleuthing ways. When the fence wagon would come in from Texline, bringing the mail, old Billy would watch to see whether the driver was new. If he was, Billy would mount the wagon, take the seat beside the driver, and before the driver had recovered his composure, Billy would sniff out and tear into the invariable tobacco sack and help himself.

As a rule pets were discouraged as severely as alcohol. This was especially true of dogs, for cattle might mistake them for wolves and stampede. An exception was Fred Graven's Great Dane.

"He stayed in the tent or under the wagon and slept by my bed and he didn't bark at anything. He knew his place. He rode on the wagon seat with me as we moved from camping place to camping place. The only times that he showed off as a dog was when we went into Texline and Channing. There he went up one street and down another whipping every dog in the town and having all the women folks after him with a club. He certainly stood in with the cow outfit."

Not calculated to stampede, but every bit as noisy as any bleating goat or barking dog, was a talking match that took place at a roundup in the late 1880's. Decades later auditors were still marveling at it, long after they had forgotten any other details of the roundup. It came about when Dick Pincham, a boss of one of the two wagon crews working for the Buffalo Springs Division, boasted that he had "the outtalkingest man on the roundup." J. M. Curry remembers the contest went like this:

"The Cimarron crowd disputed it and offered to back Fred Hollister against all comers; consequently Pincham called up Bill Coats and they called Hollister and they were introduced and told what they were expected to do and that no holts were barred.

"Hollister seemed somewhat surprised that he should be entered in a talking match, but Coats, realizing the advantage of a surprise attack, fired into him and talked a blue streak for a few minutes. But finally Hollister says, 'Hold on here— let's get down and make our beds so we can talk with some satisfaction.' Accordingly they got down, unsaddled, and staked out their horses, spread their saddle blankets, using their saddles for pillows, commenced talking. But it soon became apparent that Hollister had the staying qualities.

"This was about the time the phonograph was invented, and they was all the talk at this time, but no one here had ever seen one or knew how they worked, but everybody called them talking machines. So when Coats seen he had no chance he gasped for breath a few times like he was choking, got up, and backed up a few steps and drawed a long breath, and turned to the crowd and said, 'Gentlemen, I am willing to talk against any man, but I refuse to talk against machinery.' This ended the talking match."

"This" also ends this chapter.

"We never knew whether he was drowned or not"

AFTERWARDS

SEVERAL THINGS have always puzzled me. What, for instance, becomes of all the fashionable, popular dogs when they are no longer fashionable and popular? And what is the fate of romantic young crooners when they are fifty and hoarse and physically slack? Such a list could continue at some length, but one group that has never been included in such puzzling is the old cowboy. He follows all sorts of logical trails until he can no longer ride down the road of life. The XIT hands were no exception. Let's follow a few of them.

As a start, John Durks of Glendive became an engineer for the Northern Pacific Railroad. A coworker of his, thirty years before, on the XIT spread in Montana was Bill Coats, the champion talker who was dethroned by an alleged human talking machine. Bill Coats had helped boss the first herd into Montana. Three decades later he was still a cowhand, working for the Mussellshell. On the other hand, their whilom ranch master, Ab Owings, had become an independent ranch owner near the Dakota line, only to be felled by a bolt of lightning. Al and Linn Boyce also developed their own Montana ranches, as did L. D. McMakin near Fallon. Mammoth Bob Fudge had his spread on the Little Powder till a horse fell on him, breaking his hip. Fudge died of gangrene.

Henry Eubanks, foreman at Rito Blanco in the 1890's, turned away from ranching, becoming a county judge in Channing. Eubanks was remembered kindly by the hands because he had two eligible daughters, though he personally disagreed as to their eligibility, particularly when his Lulu was mentioned. The cowboys joked frequently that any man who packed a white-handled six gun or sang "My Lulu Gal" wouldn't last long on Rito Blanco!

When in later years Bob Beverly became an inspector for cattlemen's associations and sanitary boards in Texas and New Mexico, he found that the old jibes by outsiders still pursued him and other XIT men. Whenever their association with the giant spread was mentioned, someone was sure to spit and jeer, "Montgomery Ward punchers!" Beverly also found that two decades after he had died, A. G. Boyce, the general manager, continued to be roundly hated by marginal cowmen. Beverly himself was not blindly loyal to his former boss but rather objective in his approach:

"He would have made a good governor of the state of Texas or any other state. He not only knew cattle but he knew men . . . ; he was a good business man; he knew what to do with cattle on the range, what to do with them on the trail, and when they needed to go to market.

"A. G. Boyce was my friend, although I didn't know it, and the more he thought of a cowpuncher the more he put on him to do, and tried to see if he could burn him down, and get a lot of cowpuncher fool ideas out of his head.

"A. G. Boyce would never send any man back to a division . . . where the ranch Boss had discharged him from, but if he thought the man was entitled to another trial, he would get some of the other division bosses to give him a chance. He asked me not to quit the ranch when I did, and told me to go to Chicago with a train of cattle and get over my mad spell, and, as I and John Armstrong were good friends, to come back and stay with John until such time as he could see fit to give me a better job, and told me that jobs was going to be hard to land in the spring, but I never went back to the ranch until after he had passed away twenty years afterwards, but I made a mistake."

On the other hand Beverly thought that Boyce made a mistake by remaining too long at the XIT.

"He nearly controlled that part of the Panhandle, and it gave him too much power, and like all men given excessive power, it has a tendency to make them more or less oppressive, and less inclined to make allowances for the other fellow."

Boyce was a participant in one reversal of fortune that had its ironic side. A. H. Webb, later an early sheriff of Dallam County in Texas, had been in the Confederate army. After Lee's surrender he had left Tennessee and ridden a mule into West Texas, where he made a fortune in ranching, as well as gaining some notoriety by being aboard that first train that Sam Bass and Joel Collins held up.

According to Beverly, among Webb's employes in the 1880's was Boyce, who trailed cattle for him. But the vagaries of cattle fortunes were such that in 1893–1894 Webb was broke and Boyce was bossing the largest ranch in the nation.

Webb did not hesitate to look up his old employe, who promptly hired his erstwhile employer as division boss at Buffalo Springs.

Physically, cowboys were a poor risk. A horse might be a hand's best friend, but possibly as many cowboys lost their lives to horses as owed them. Uncle Jack Leonard, who had freighted for Custer and somehow escaped the Little Big Horn massacre, worked with cattle until a horse fell back on him and ended his riding forever. Back to freighting went Uncle Jack, an old man in body, gnarled but "tough as a boot [with] a temper . . . vitriolic towards humans but gentle to animals. . . . I do not believe he was afraid of God, man, or devil, the things on earth, in the sky, or things underground," writes Edward MacConnell, who confesses that he himself was a better guitar player than cowboy.

Uncle Jack was still at his freighting in his seventies, a man who had survived the Civil War and Indian skirmishes, who had guided emigrant wagon trains, and who was revered as a living link with Western history. When Bob Duke took over as XIT general manager, he felt, in Frank Shardelman's words, that "the camping out was too rugged for Uncle Jack in bad weather and told him he had better stay around Rito Blanco. Uncle Jack refused and said, 'What do you want to make of me now? A barn yard savage?' Bob laughed and said to me, 'I guess it is up to you, Frank, to take care of him.' He was rugged and went through the winter fine. I would load the heavy freight, but he never would ask any favors."

Noted equally for his bull-headedness and for his high-pitched cussing, Uncle Jack died typically and with his boots on. He had driven out from Tascosa, where once he had won two corner lots in a poker game and swapped them for two quarts of whiskey, and had run into a howling norther. He was found on the prairie, frozen to death. Apparently with his last strength he had cut the traces of his team and checked out.

All sorts of men passed through the corral. Where some came from, the men never knew and seldom asked. Where others went, they never bothered to find out. In some instances they did not remember their range-riding partner's name, if indeed they had ever known it to begin with. One of the nameless was an Englishman, who in J. W. Standifer's words, was learning "the cow business from the bottom up."

"He smoked expensive cigars, and at first he'd pass them around, but that soon got old; so he got to where he'd sit up and smoke by himself. He was a smart man and well educated. The boys often held kangaroo court. They were a little shy about including him. He remarked to someone that he didn't feel like one of the boys unless they whipped him too. So they ganged up on him and liked to have whipped the seat of his pants out.

"Some said he talked with a brogue, and he said it was us that had the brogue not him. One day he got a letter from home saying his uncle had 'flopped his wings' as he put it, leaving him a lot of money. So he pulled up and started for his homeland. He just about had time to reach Galveston when they had the awful flood. We never knew whether he was drowned or not.

" 'Maryland' was also a unique character. I don't ever remember having heard his real name; he hailed from Maryland, so 'Maryland' he became.*

"Also among our cowboy charcters was Fidel Trujillo, a Mexican. He had a trick horse named Dealer, a brown horse with stocking legs and bald face. He had taught him to pitch

---

* It was Maryland who astonished the hands his first night in the bunkhouse by kneeling by his bedroll to pray. "And not a man said a word or made a sound," remembers Standifer; "in his simple faith he was their superior."

and ever time the wagon had company, especially if it were women, Fidel always made 'Dealah,' as he called him, show off."

Other than ranching, the most likely post-cowboy career for an XIT hand was as some sort of peace officer. Ira Aten was sheriff of Castro County; Rufe Morris became a guard at the Montana state prison at Deer Lodge.

One boy, who stayed only long enough to be known as Brown, spent the summer of 1898 hauling wood to the various branding pens. Later, it was rumored, he went to work for a railroad, became a fireman, stuck his head out of the cab looking for signals, and cracked it against a water tank.

When years later Mrs. Duke picked up the trail of an old XIT hand, John G. Lang, he wrote her from Haines, Oregon:

"I would like to come to the XIT reunion but I am an old sour-dough prospector and must do my assessment work on my mining claims. I have never got a dollar out of the mine but I am *only seventy-five*; so I still have hopes."

Fred Graven, who emerged from the Missouri woods in 1893 to work with cattle to 1951, had the same lack of economic luck. After the XIT sold its cattle in 1912, Graven cooked for the Hitch Ranch in Oklahoma before moving down to the giant Scottish-owned Matador Ranch in Texas for five years. When the 1918 "flu"* caught him, he spent some time hospitalized, in the only official visit he ever made to a hospital. It left him deep in debt.

To recoup, Graven turned to a hated job, skinning cows. With his partner he would work all day and skin at night.

"This man and I had only moonlight nights on which to skin cattle, and how the coyotes did howl up on the points of

---

* That same winter was as difficult for cattle as it was for human beings. As Hiram Sweeney used to say, "I owned a ranch and cattle, but that winter made a hired man out of me."

canyons. Every once in a while a loafer [lobo] gave his hair-raising howl. He wasn't after carcasses, as the coyotes were, but would kill some cow that was down. He had to have his meat fresh.

"After a hard day's work gathering and feeding poor cows, we would go to skinning the dead ones. This man A—— and I were goaded on to do it. I skinned to pay my hospital bills and he skinned to get married, and so we thought we could do any hard work.

"I used to be ready to take a social glass but working with the XIT and the Matador ranches, I got away from that long ago. My strong drink now is coffee."

Ed Faubion, who started life down in Central Texas, covered most of western North America before he hung up his spurs for the last time. His story is told succinctly in the third person by his wife:

"When Ed Faubion arrived in Amarillo, he was eighteen years old. He wore a very cheap suit of clothes and was far from strong, as he had had a siege of pneumonia. Mr. Boyce looked him over and said: 'I knew your father; you should have some good timber in you. Take this card, get you some warm clothes, and give the card to Henry Boyce [A. G.'s son and ranch bookkeeper] and he will give you a job.' So he did and worked there four years. Ed made a real cowhand. He was always full of fun and thereby caused some trouble by spreading his 'loop.'

"Elliston told him and Ira Morris, his main pal to 'quit roping the cattle,' but they couldn't quit. One day Ed roped and rolled a big cow. Elliston put him and Ira on day herd for a week, for the cow's leg was broken when she hit the ground. They did not mind dayherding, for they could rope cattle every day when out of sight of the wagon.

"One day they had just roped and saddled a big steer

when Elliston rode over a hill and saw them. He told Ed, 'Go ahead. I want to see you ride him.'

" 'Oh, no,' Ed replied, 'It's Ira's time to ride him.' So he rode the steer, and Elliston was so amused he failed to fire them. He told them to come back in the spring and he would give them some work then. He was writing their checks and as Ed walked over to get his, he said, 'How would you like a camp for the winter.' Of course Ed told him that he would like that fine. So he gave him old North Camp, far from any neighbors and lonely in the extreme. But Ed stuck it out all winter. Elliston told Ed to 'take a gun over there, as the last boy that stayed there was run off by some Mexicans that wanted to use the grass.'

"On the door of this one-room house was written these words:

Good-bye, old Camp Repentance, old echoless walls farewell. Life is too short for your comfort and solitude. I've heard the wolves howl at your threshold. The windmill blew to pieces. I seen it and fell on the floor. I'm dying from tears and dyspepsia, caused from eating sow bosom and beans. I've nothing to wear but a necktie and a worthless pair of jeans.

"After four years here, the next spring he went to work for the CCC Cattle Company at Goodwell, Oklahoma, for four years; was transferred to Wilcox, Arizona, where they had a large ranch.

"Here he met a man who told him he had a large mine in Alaska. He got seventeen of the boys to sign up for transportation there, among them was the man's brother-in-law. They had to each put up a $1,000.00 into the venture. They sailed gaily away from Seattle for Nome, Alaska, in the fall of 1900.

"When they reached Nome after a stormy voyage, one

night an officer came and told them that their leader had been robbed. They went to his hotel and found him with clothes torn off and room in a very dishevelled condition. The leader's name was Mulligan.

"Ed became suspicious that it was a 'phony' robbery, for Mulligan had told him the night before, 'Ed, we could have a big time on this money, couldn't we?'

" ' You havn't got that money on your person, have you?'

" 'Oh, yes, right here in a money belt around my waist,' he said.

"So a detective sifted the ashes in the stove and found all the buttons off Mulligan's shirt in them, a thread was hanging from Mulligan's overcoat. He ripped the lining loose and found most of the money there, the remainder they found under a loosened brick in the sidewalk. The officers told the seventeen men that if they weighted Mulligan with rocks and threw him in the bay that night it would be only too good for him. But they let him go, as they were only too glad to get most of their money back.

"They formed their own company and staked out claims, but could only pan about $3.00 a day, which about covered their expenses. They stayed there until their money was about exhausted and then headed for home. Ed Faubion arrived in Seattle broke but for a $50.00 check. Only one boy stayed in Alaska of the seventeen that went there. They offered to pay his way back to the 'states' but he told them that he did not have anything but what he had there, and he would stay until he found more. They left him chopping cord wood. Years later he struck it rich and sold his claim for $2,000,000.00.

"Ed Faubion found work skinning mules on an irrigation ditch in Washington. Worked there until he got crippled by a large carbuncle on his heel, went to San Francisco and saw Mr. Vail, one of the owners of the CCC. He gave him a pass to Wilcox and his old job. He went back to punching cattle there, and later paid a visit to home folks in Lampasas County, met and married Pearl Higgins on September, 1904. He filed on a claim in New Mexico near Logan in 1907. Later went back to Texas and worked on ranches until 1922. He was working for Charley Kilgore at his north camp near Dumas. Was hurt roping cattle to brand one day. Lived only eight months after this. His wife and two brothers carried him back to his old home at Lampasas, where he died April 2, 1923. He had bought a place just before this north of Clayton. His wife still lives there. She married Leck Burk of Clayton in 1926."

When, years later, R. M. Dudley was asked for his reminiscences, he echoed the wish of so many old-timers that he could return and relive some of his past on the XIT, "but none of us would want to relive it all. Many accidents, dangers, and other disagreeable features would be no temptation. . . ."

"Some received broken legs, some broken arms, and broken collar bones seemed to be one of the very common occurrences. For myself I fell heir to a broken left hand, which gave me plenty of pain and annoyance, and the knot on the back of the hand still shows clearly. Ed Jones, another XIT man I knew, got what was worse—a broken neck—and passed on to his last resting place. Ed, however, got his neck broken the year following his work with the XIT and not while in their employ.

"I was working in the outfit on the Bravo Division when a horse fell on and rolled over John Sharp, from which he died ten days later in an Amarillo Sanitarium without ever regaining consciousness. This happened in the fall of 1898.

"Powder and lead and bad whiskey also caused the deaths of some of the old-time cowboys. But why bring that up? They are gone from us never again to return. It was an iron-clad rule with the XIT that no one in their employ should drink or gamble, but some did so anyway, only to lose their job immediately if found out. . . . Best for all concerned if all companies had been as strict."

Several times Arch Sneed tried to quit the XIT to work for the Cherry Cattle Company in Arizona. Always A. G. Boyce, who "had a kind of fatherly way about him with his men and was rough in his language in giving advice," dissauded him. Once Colonel Boyce told Sneed that he was the right age "and had about little enough sense to go down there and get strung in with a bunch of rustlers and wind up hanging to a tree or be put in the penitentiary." Again Sneed was persuaded to stay.

But finally in late November, 1905, Sneed tried again, and this time he made the break.

"I entered the service of the Rock Island on the first day of December, 1905, . . . and went to work in the roundhouse as helper. I went to firing the following spring and was promoted to engineer in April, 1913, and have never missed a pay day to this date, although I have drawed some very small ones."

W. A. Askew experienced all the XIT had to offer, from haying on the Rito Blanco to rounding up horses on the Bovina. Once, out with a companion named Hunt, he arrived at Alamositas Camp to find no one home. With no cook, Askew made a valiant, if distasteful, effort:

"We had a sack of flour, and a bucket of lard, and salt and pepper, and no beds, or suggins of any kind. I told my friend Jo Hunt that I was a good cook and that I would dish him up a mess that he would never forget. I mixed flour and water together and some salt and pepper to make it taste just right. I boiled it until I thought the flour had all congealed with the water, salt, and pepper, and we poured some of the stuff out in tincups and drank it. We had the same concoction for breakfast.

"Next morning I saddled the same old horse I rode away from ranch headquarters. I had about fifteen miles to go where I was to turn back, and my friend Mr. Hunt take the horses on to Bovina headquarters. We had gone about three miles and found the cowboys building corrals. We stopped and got a good breakfast and visited, as I had never seen any of them before.

"Once we branded eight thousand calves and cows on the Bravo Division for Ed Halsell; we branded fifteen hundred on the Escarbada Division. We had these cows and calves about three or four miles from the Bravo Division at dark one afternoon; Bob Duke was in charge; he said to the boys, 'If you get these cows and calves across the fence, you will not have to stand guard tonight.' It was raining at the time, and the next morning, we had about one half of them on *the other side of the fence.* It rained and hailed and lightninged and thundered, and we were all wet and hungry at sunup the next morning.

"I had smelled the sweat; I had tasted the salty grime from the silt and dust of the trailing herd; I had fought my way to the top of my mount and I was all over him as he zigzagged, fence-rowed, and changed directions.

"I saw the pointers taking their places, in front, the swing men coming up to take their places, and the flankers and drag men coming after. I had seen the old bowlegged dust-be-grimed riders of the Old West, remnant of both sides in the Civil War, which is now told in story, song, legend, and tra-dition with their ten-gallon hats, their flannel shirts, boots and spurs, and six guns. Their coil of rope, ragged chaps, and wornout slickers, and the old chuck wagon was my home for a long time.

"I have ridden the cayuse, which had a belligerent dispo-sition, I have helped the boys in a kangaroo court, and seen a tenderfoot tried and ready to be hanged, and a friendly cowboy come to his help with a flourishing gun and the boys scatter.

"I was a cowhand looking for adventure, and I found it on the XIT Ranch, the largest ranch in the world under fence, 3,000,000 acres of land, 200,000 head of cattle and probably 10,000 head of horses. I have helped to cross a herd over a swollen stream, tying the chuck wagon to the running gears and the cowhands tying their ropes to the wagon and helping pull across, and sometimes by raft."

But like so many others, Askew reached the day when he was ready to move into a different life. He quit the XIT, attended business college, and went into business for himself. When he was fifty-seven years old Askew received his license to practice law, having studied at home nights for four years, frequently till three o'clock in the morning. When last he wrote Mrs. Duke he was seventy-one years old, had a dozen years as an attorney behind him, and "have a very good practice now."

The list is studded with boys who made good. They peopled the several counties of West Texas and eastern New Mexico with judges, sheriffs, and county clerks. Allen Willbanks became a banker and oil man. When W. O.—or Bill, as he started out—Culbertson died in the spring of 1959, his obituary was carried in newspapers all over the Southwest because he owned five large ranches in the three states of Texas, New Mexico, and Colorado; he had developed a tick resistant beef cross strain; and, most dear to old XIT men, who liked to take on a running fight in general and one with the government in particular, he had fought the Internal Revenue Service for seven years before the United States Supreme Court declared him victor in an $80,000 income-tax suit.

And so they came and they went, cowboys on the largest range under fence in the world. They came as boys, they

came as men. They went away, touched by the spaciousness
of life on the XIT. Taciturn or talkative, cynical or cheerful,
they joined together to grow sentimental about the days when
they rode through 100,000-acre pastures toward horizons
without limit or break. And one of them at least, Arch Sneed,
didn't even wait to grow old to become nostalgic—

"I left Buffalo Springs on September 22, 1904, sold my
bed to one of the boys, rode one of my horses known as J. B.
Clark to Farwell Park, and took the train for Channing to
get my time. I sacked my saddle at the station, put it in a
gunny sack, and checked it as baggage, turned old J. B. Clark
loose one mile from the XIT camp. As he trotted away towards camp I watched him, and I have to admit these thirty-
three years later that I remember of having shed tears when I
realized I was severing my connection with the Buffalo
Springs Division, as I had experienced some of the happiest
days of my life during my stay there, and it seemed more
like home to me than any place I had lived after leaving
home."

Out on the open prairie they slept, or squinted to see herds
of antelopes through hazy mirages, or listened to the coyote
lift his mournful, lonesome serenade to the moon, or caught
catfish in the clear-running Cold Water, or pitted their horse
savvy against wild mustangs. Whatever their tastes in work
or diversion, they could all have agreed with J. S. Kenyon,
who summed up his feeling for the huge old ranch in these
words:
It is a grand place to view the stars.

Or with Charlie Burrus, when he wrote:

The boy that came out there and thought there was nothing to
do but sit astraddle of a horse, did not usually stay long.

Appendix

Horses Remembered by XIT Men

The following horses are mentioned in these reminiscences and are listed here for nostalgic, as well as indexing, reasons:

Index